Mystical Insights for Personal Growth

WHERE
THE HEAVENS
KISS
THE EARTH

RABBI KARMI INGBER

BALBOA.
PRESS
A DIVISION OF HAY HOUSE

Balboa Press books may be ordered through booksellers or by contacting:

Balboa Press
A Division of Hay House
1663 Liberty Drive
Bloomington, IN 47403
www.balboapress.com
1 (877) 407-4847

Because of the dynamic nature of the Internet, any web addresses or links contained in this book may have changed since publication and may no longer be valid. The views expressed in this work are solely those of the author and do not necessarily reflect the views of the publisher, and the publisher hereby disclaims any responsibility for them.

The author of this book does not dispense medical advice or prescribe the use of any technique as a form of treatment for physical, emotional, or medical problems without the advice of a physician, either directly or indirectly. The intent of the author is only to offer information of a general nature to help you in your quest for emotional and spiritual well-being. In the event you use any of the information in this book for yourself, which is your constitutional right, the author and the publisher assume no responsibility for your actions.

Any people depicted in stock imagery provided by Thinkstock are models, and such images are being used for illustrative purposes only. Certain stock imagery © Thinkstock.

Print information available on the last page.

ISBN: 978-1-5043-6087-6 (sc)
ISBN: 978-1-5043-6089-0 (hc)
ISBN: 978-1-5043-6088-3 (e)

Library of Congress Control Number: 2016912457

Balboa Press rev. date: 03/13/2017

לכבוד אשת חיל'

In Honor of a Righteous
Woman of Valor

Yulishka Shulamit bas Esther Abigail

לעילוי נשמות

In loving memory of

Yechezkel (Harry) Ingber

לעילוי נשמות

In loving memory of

Sol and Sarah Sachs

לעילוי נשמות

In loving memory of

Rivka and Gedalya Steinmetz

לעילוי נשמות

In loving memory of

Leonard and Sylvia Rothstein

לעילוי נשמות

In loving memory of

Irving and Toby Schwartz

CONTENTS

APPROBATIONS

Dear Friends,

I have read the manuscript of "Where the Heavens Kiss the Earth" by my esteemed friend and colleague Rabbi Karmi Ingber. Rabbi Ingber has produced a comprehensive study of the foundations of Torah philosophy. He presents the issues of the meaning of life, the existence of good and evil, free-will and G-d's omnipotence, the physical and spiritual realms, and this world and the world to come. This is not a book to be casually read but rather a presentation to be carefully studied. The author draws from the vast and deep classical sources and gives over a lucid and well developed understanding of these issues. He utilizes down to earth examples and pithy anecdotes to illustrate complicated ideas and make them more comprehensible. He also provides practical exercises to enable one to transform these abstract ideas into the reality of one's everyday living.

I commend Rabbi Ingber for this masterful work and recommend it to all those that want to make life's journey in this world more meaningful, significant, and purposeful.

May the Almighty grant Rabbi Ingber and his family life and health to continue to merit the community in many varied ways.

Sincerely,
With Torah Blessings,
Rabbi Zev Leff

RABBI SIMCHA SCHEINBERG
Rosh HaYeshiva Yeshivas Torah Ore

הרב שמחה שיינברג
ראש הישיבה, ישיבת תורה אור ירושלים
בן מרן רבי חיים פינחס שיינברג זצוק"ל

בס"ד

אלול תשע"ו

זה היום נגילה ונשמחה ביום היגלות אור ספר "היכא דנשקי שמיא וארעא" ע"י הרב כרמי דוד אינגבר שליט"א אשר זכה לשבת בבית מדרשינו ישיבת "תורה אור", וזכה לשמש בסברא אצל מרן שר התורה אאמו"ר הגאון הגדול מרן רבי חיים פינחס שיינברג זצוקלל"ה, וינק מתורתו של האי כלי חמדה לשון הממהר באמרי שפר גיסי הגאון הגדול רבי חיים דוב אלטוסקי זצוק"ל [בעמח"ס חידושי בתרא] ויגע בהתמדה גדולה ועלה בתורה ויר"ש עד שנהיה לגברא רבה, ובספר זה רואים שנכתב מתוך עמל ויגיעה הרבה.

והנני בזה להביע את שמחתי כי יצא לנו דבר טוב ואין טוב אלא תורה, מלב מלא תורה ויראת ה'.

ואין לי אלא לברכו שימשיך בהרבצת תורה להעמיד תלמידים כיד ה' הטובה עליו ויזכה בספרו זה לקרב את אחינו בני ישראל אל אבינו שבשמים

הכו"ח לכבוד התורה ולומדיה

שמחה בן אאמו"ר הגאון הגדול
מרן רבי חיים פינחס זצוק"ל
שיינברג

הרב שמחה שיינברג * ראש הישיבה * ישיבת תורה אור
קרית מטרסדורף ירושלים

6 Panim Merot Street• Jerusalem, PO Box 6967 • 02.537.2928
רחוב פנים מאירות 6 ירושלים ת.ד. 6979 טל.02.537.2928 ישראל

Rabbi Yitzchak Berkovits
Sanhedria HaMurchevet 113/27
Jerusalem, Israel 97707
02-5813847

יצחק שמואל הלוי ברקוביץ
ראש רשת הכוללים לינת הצדק
סנהדרי'ה המורחבת 113/27
ירושלם ת"ו

Bs"D Jerusalem 10 Elul, 5776

Rabbi Karmi Ingber has invested a significant portion of his time and efforts in researching and teaching central issues in Jewish thought, and is now making them available for the masses in this comprehensive work.

Where the Heavens Kiss the Earth presents complicated areas in Jewish Philosophy in a clear, pleasant and rational manner, that can be easily understood by all who wish to. It is easy to read and enjoyable, yet so profound and accurate.

I cannot help but remember Rabbi Ingber's classes at Ner Le'elef and at The Jerusalem Kollel years ago, where students confronted some of the more difficult concepts in Judaism through a mass of carefully chosen source material. In this work Rabbi Ingber draws from those sources and brings them down to attitudes in our daily lives.

This book is a wonderful resource for all who study and teach Jewish thought, and could be life changing for the questioning individual.

It is my hope that this work will make its way to the homes and hearts of people worldwide, and will inspire them to live the beauty of an authentic, meaningful and spiritual life. May the author continue to educate our brethren in person and in print for many years to come.

Sincerely,

FOREWORD

In order to better understand this work and its author, one first needs to get to know Rabbi Ingber's shul, the Kehilla. Rabbi Ingber leads the Kehilla as a rabbi and spiritual guide. There, his unique leadership and Torah wisdom come to life. One who visits our shul might be surprised that hidden away in the suburbs of Atlanta, surrounded by Georgian pines and seemingly endless shopping centers and neighborhoods, is a hidden treasure of spiritual growth and Torah study. Those who have visited our community-from across America and all over the world-will testify that they instantly felt like they had just gained a new family. People searching for spirituality are drawn to this oasis and are welcomed with open arms. At the Kehilla, we explore Judaism at our own pace and in our own way. Guests often express surprise at how we come together every Shabbos for communal meals and other bonding activities at our shul. Rabbi Ingber leads this beautiful edifice of a Torah true community that is based on kindness, a passion for truth seeking, and a genuine love for every person.

In many ways, Rabbi Ingber leads our shul by studying the holy Torah with diligence and passion. When he shares Torah insights with us, he teaches from the heart and focuses on reaching each of us personally, to help us with our own struggles and spiritual growth. Rabbi Ingber cares about every person who walks in the doors of his shul. Everyone knows instantly that they count and are valued as a part of our community. This atmosphere of belonging has developed in large part through Rabbi Ingber's connection to the Torah and his emphasis on its most essential teachings: unity -*achdut* - and unconditional love - *ahavah bli sibah*.

Rabbi Ingber's classes and talks also draw a lot of their power and effectiveness from his vast knowledge of mysticism and *Chassidut*, the inner dimensions of Torah. Throughout my years as a student of Rabbi Ingber and a member of the Kehilla, I have admired the way that Rabbi Ingber has applied the mystical dimensions of Torah to everyday lessons that at once draw the heart closer to God while guiding the pulse of our community.

As I have grown closer to Rabbi Ingber over the past few years as his student, I have grown tremendously in my connection to the Torah, not only by receiving his wisdom but also by observing his love of learning. Rabbi Ingber has also taught me the great importance of joy, song, friendship, humor, and fun as integral aspects of growing closer to God. Most importantly, Rabbi Ingber has taught all of us at the Kehilla to strive to live by the foundational statement of Rabbi Akivah: *Love your friend as yourself. This is the great principle of the Torah.*

I feel I am a better person for observing, week by week, Rabbi Ingber's love and respect for every person and how he offers unconditional guidance and support to everyone. I have watched him over the years form bonds with each of us, and guide us on the straight path of *halachah* with a rare mixture of compassion, thorough knowledge, and common sense. I am always amazed that Rabbi Ingber will give hours of his time every week to counsel people with his spiritual knowledge and his understanding of psychology, in order to lift people out of the darkness of their difficulties and back to the light of joy through Judaism. I also personally appreciate the many hours Rabbi Ingber has spent with me, whether offering me advice for my own personal struggles, or learning the deepest sources of mysticism and *Chassidut*.

Rabbi Ingber shines as a spiritual leader with an approach to learning and leadership rare to find in today's society. He genuinely cares about helping every individual. His inspiring services, with song and dance, open people up to experience *simchas hachaim*, the joy of the spiritual life. Rabbi Ingber's speaking style is an enthralling experience, weaving lofty concepts with drama and humor. His teachings reflect his broad knowledge base with a specialty in mysticism, spirituality and personal growth. He combines Torah knowledge with psychology, music, meditation (including his hobby of Tai Chi) and human understanding to allow people from all walks of life to experience the beauty and grandeur of Torah. Everybody who reads this book can feel his embrace to enhance their own spiritual path.

Michael Kleinman, Esq.

INTRODUCTION

The most significant issues in life are often the most difficult to comprehend. Understanding our purpose, destiny, free-will and suffering are crucial to comprehending and appreciating the patterns of our lives. And yet we may often receive only superficial clichés and pat answers for our questions. But because of the depth of these concerns, concepts and challenges, there are no simple answers. Very little in our lives fits into neat little boxes; something always seems to stick out. The truth is not always obvious and a deeper level of understanding will be necessary to comprehend these issues; something that is beyond our limited perception.

Our limited perception is one of the reasons we may find statements of our Sages that appear contradictory to our untrained eyes. This challenge does not only affect the uninitiated; it also plagues the knowledgeable. During my ten years of training Rabbis in Israel who were preparing to take communal roles overseas, I was surprised to see how many well educated, spiritually enlightened people were not clear on the details of these vital topics.

The purpose of writing this book was to try and clearly lay out the fundamental concepts of spirituality in an easily understood and consistent format.

Using the explanations of our great Sages, I have tried to resolve apparent inconsistencies by presenting the deeper underlying themes. However, as is the nature of these ideas, my explanation is also limited and can be further enhanced by the questioning of piercing minds and more spiritually elevated individuals than myself. The ability to contain endless concepts in a finite form is only possible for the Endless Creator. This objective has been replicated by people of great spiritual prowess who have accessed Divine inspiration for their explanation of the limitless.

I do not profess to have these abilities. My goal here is simply to translate these deep concepts into terminology and analogies that can be understood by everyone. And in light of this, I have tried to tailor this book toward two seemingly incongruous audiences, the beginner and the advanced. My deepest hope is that when a spiritual seeker will want to enter into the realms of spirituality, both a beginner and an advanced student will be able to use this book as a guide to consolidate, assimilate and deepen their knowledge to clearly understand the philosophical and spiritual systems of the Torah.

The concepts and explanations presented here are not my own. They have all been gleaned from the wealth of spiritual sources we have access to. I have culled from this rich wellspring, sometimes even using a particular phrase based on a teaching of our great masters. Any mistakes or misunderstandings are solely mine as the sources are well beyond my grasp.

The citing and quotes were too numerous to mention, and I have not attempted to list them all. I have made extensive use of the primary Judaic sources including the Tanach, Talmud, Midrash and Zohar and the teaching of our great Sages: the *Geonim, Rishonim* and *Achronim,* and in particular I have used the teachings of the masters of *chassidus, machshavah, kabbalah* and *mussar.* These include the Arizal, Rabbi Chaim Vital, the Ramchal, the Maharal, the Vilna Gaon, Rabbi Chaim Volozhin, the Baal Hatanya, Rabbi Tzaddok HaCohen, the Shem Meshmuel, Rabbi Eliyahu Eliezer Dessler, Rabbi Yisroel Salanter, the Leshem, the Gesher Hachayim, and many more. Additionally, I have incorporated the ideas and lessons I have learned from my teachers, Rabbis, friends and colleagues. These include but are not limited to Rabbi Zev Leff, Rabbi Moshe Shapiro, Rabbi Daniel Belsky, Rabbi

Dovid Gottlieb, Rabbi Beryl Gershonfeld, Rabbi M. Goldstein, my Rebbe of blessed memory Rabbi Chaim Dov Altusky, *ztz'l* and my Rosh Yeshiva of blessed memory, Rabbi Chaim Pinchas Scheinberg, *ztz'l*. All are certainly to be credited for my access and understanding of Torah thought.

This book is entitled *Where the Heavens Kiss the Earth*, which refers to the mystical teaching about the point from where the world emanates, the spot on the Temple Mount where our prayer ascends to the Heavens. This is the mystical place where the male and female dimensions of creation meet, where we most connect with the infinite in this world. The title is also based on my objective to bring lofty concepts down into common parlance and the modern milieu. The subtitle of this book: *Mystical Insights for Personal Growth*, relates to the second purpose of this text, which is translating knowledge into action and using mystical wisdom to enhance our lives.

Our Sages exhort us to act upon the knowledge that we know. To help incorporate these Torah concepts into our daily lives, I have added practical applications at the end of every chapter. The actualization of life compels us to act in the physical world with the mental conceptions we internalize. So it is my sincerest hope that the exercises at the end of each chapter will help us to transform the information we gain in each chapter into lessons of practical benefit.

After these applications, there are also additional notes that add or clarify information within the chapters that was not included in the initial discussion.

I would like to thank my teachers, students, friends and family that have inspired and educated me on many of these issues as well as my editor Chava Dumas, manuscript advisor Joseph Skibell, author of Six Memos from the *Last Millennium: A Novelist Reads the Talmud* and numerous other works, as well as my publishers and distributors that have done an amazing job bringing this book to life.

I also want to thank our awesome, warm and loving community in Atlanta, Georgia, the Kehilla, where everyone is inspired to grow spiritually in a unique and individual way.

Endless thanks to my beautiful, loving and supportive wife, Elisheva, and to my wonderful children, grandchildren and my dear mother.

And most of all, I want to give thanks and praise to the Source of all life, Who has given me everything. And Who has given me all that I know, as a gift of kindness from His endless Torah.

CHAPTER ONE

A WORLD OF PURPOSE

....

What are the most important questions we need answered in our lives?

If we think about it, we realize that our questions have been asked before, grappled with by philosophers and writers, and are called the existential questions: Why are we here? What is the meaning of life? Most thinking people have asked themselves these questions in their youth. The bizarre part is that although we never got a satisfactory answer, we usually just moved on with life, never thinking about the issues again, except maybe at some traumatic moment or literally on our deathbeds.

But the answers to these questions are not really optional. It's not like being curious about comets or rainbows and if we don't sate our curiosity life continues without this information. We are not informed, but we manage. By definition, if we don't know why we are alive and why we are here, it becomes impossible to live correctly.

Purpose as Opposed to 'Meaning'

Imagine I gave a primitive tribesman a Ferrari for his birthday. He has never seen a car before and he has no idea what purpose it serves. If he uses the car as an altar for his gods or even as a place to sleep, can we say that the purpose of the car has been achieved? This is the general flaw with many approaches to the existential questions, from Aristotle's intellectual approach to the modern-day layman. The definition of purpose cannot be made by the user of the item; we have to learn about it from the manufacturer! The person who designs a car does so for a reason.

This is true of all purposeful acts. If a vehicle is built for the purpose of transport, if we use it as a paper weight, it may serve some kind of function but certainly not the one it was created to do. Consequently, we can't say it has fulfilled its purpose. A Ferrari is built with 900 horsepower, aerodynamic design and engine efficiency, with speed and status. Using it as paper weight would miss the point! Similarly, if we decide on what we enjoy doing in life and what feels meaningful to us, that may not necessarily have anything to do with our true purpose.

If we saw someone who claimed that drinking beer and watching TV all day was the purpose of his life, we would think that's a tragic waste. It is obvious that a person is made to do much more than that. We sadly realize that this TV watching beer drinker is not maximizing all that he can be and he needs to know that he has more potential.

The more difficult concept to comprehend is that even if one acts nobly, without understanding the entire human being, the nature of the universe and the human role in that plan, one will never fully grasp one's own purpose.

We need to access all the information from the creator of the system who knows all the parts of the system, what every aspect represents and what purpose it serves. Without this information, we may use a Ferrari foolishly as a paperweight or with more ingenuity as a shelter, but either way, we will not be able to access the true reason and purpose for its formation.

Now you may retort, "You are implying that there is a Creator of the universe! Who said we were created at all? Maybe we are only cosmic accidents, flukes of nature."

If this was true, then I would agree that there is no greater purpose. There can't be because accidents are by definition purposeless! If I trip and spill the milk, it's foolish to ask me, "What is the purpose of putting milk on the floor?" There was no purpose, it was an accident. If the universe is a cosmic accident, it makes sense that some people would decide that the correct approach to life is to party as much as possible. This is a modern version of the old Greek adage, "Eat, drink, and be merry for tomorrow we die."

Others correctly feel that this is too shallow and meaningless and genuinely look to do things that are kind, compassionate and just. That's a huge improvement over living a life of meaninglessness. How much greater would it be to get the *inside scoop* on the deeper purpose of our existence?

We have the benefit of this vital knowledge that has been transmitted to us by the Jewish mystics throughout the ages.

We can turn to what they knew the Torah teaches us is the reason for our creation by examining the written and oral Torah, Biblical commentary and the mystical secrets conveyed in the *Kabbalah*. The written Torah refers to the twenty-four books of the Tanach which include the first five, which are called the Five Books of Moses, as well as the writings of the Prophets and masters of Divine Inspiration (*Ruach Hakodesh*). The oral Torah refers to the Talmud, Mishnah, and Midrash.

The Purpose of Creation (in a Nutshell)

According to the *Kabbalists* the purpose of creation is *to enable us to receive the ultimate and maximum pleasure.* This may surprise us and our visceral response to this is to incredulously shout, "That's absurd, it can't be!" How can we say that the purpose of creation is pleasure when we see a world that in no way guarantees pleasure for all? How can there be suffering, difficulties and death at the end of the road if the purpose of life is pleasure?

And what about those of us who are not experiencing pleasure? Are we created for no purpose?

Imagine for a moment that you were the Omnipotent Creator and wanted to give humanity the greatest pleasure. Is this how your world would look?

In my imagination, I would have every baby born with the taste of vanilla ice cream on his or her tongue. At age two the taste would segue into chocolate, and by age fifty each person would be constantly inundated with cookies and crème. An Omnipotent Creator is not bound by limitations. It's true that Baskin Robbins has only 31 wonderful flavors, but an Omnipotent Being could give us infinite flavors!

So if there's a way to give us endless pleasure without the pain, why is the world so laden with challenges and difficulties?

The Bread of Shame

The great Sage known as the *Shelah Hakadosh* reveals to us a mystical secret to help us understand this conundrum. He writes that before a human being is born, his or her soul comes before the Eternal One and experiences unfathomable pleasure basking in the Supernal Light. This pleasure is a transcendental joy greater than all possible pleasures combined in this reality. However, there is one shortcoming. This is what the mystics call *Nehama Dekisufa*, the "Bread of Shame." Although the pleasure is tremendous, it is tainted by the fact that the recipients have been passive in the process. They have done nothing to deserve the pleasure and therefore are tantamount to a parasite or a beggar. This missing piece in the integral experience of pleasure is what precipitates our need to enter this world. The Eternal wisdom dictates that a person should be brought into this multifaceted reality in order to earn his eternal connection, be the owner of its good, and thereby experience it on an entirely different plane. That is why we need to be placed in a world where good and evil envelop us, and we must successfully choose our path in a maze of confusion, enabling us to ultimately be the catalyst and cause of our own experience. (1*)

Accordingly, we can understand that in Jewish Law, the lowest form of charity is where both the recipient and benefactor are aware of the gift since that engenders embarrassment for the recipient. We can also understand that the highest form of charity is to hire someone for a job or give a loan because it keeps the recipient's honor intact. When the one who gives a loan receives it back, the receiver can say, "Thank you. Here is your loan back. With this loan I was able to invest in a business, and the money I've made, I earned!" This is a completely different experience than being a passive recipient of charity.

The Holy Tongue

This concept is revealed in the actual Hebrew alphabet. We have a *Kabbalistic* principle that the universe was created through the Holy Tongue. (2*) This means that unlike other languages which are constructed through human consensus to identify objects and actions with certain sounds, *Lashon Hakodesh*, the Holy Language, is integral in the actual formation of the objects themselves! The letters and sounds are the building blocks of the creation, like atoms combining to create molecules and amino acids uniting to form proteins. Accordingly, every letter, in its sound, form, numerology and meaning, as well as the words which are created through the combinations of letters, has incredible depth and significance. (3*)

Our present discussion can be grasped by studying the third and fourth letters of the Hebrew Alphabet, *Gimmel* and *Dalet* respectively. The literal meaning of the letter *Gimmel* is a "giver," as in the phrase *Gommel Chasadim*, one who *gives* kindness. If we look at the form of the *Gimmel*, we are even able to distinguish some of the traits of the giver himself.

Notice how the "leg'" of the *Gimmel* ג is extended forward. (Hebrew moves from right to left.) This represents the "giver" (*Gommel*) actively running out to find the needy. The definition of a giver is not someone who gives when asked, but rather someone who fervently and constantly seeks out opportunities to give.

Now the *Gimmel* is figuratively giving to the next letter in the system which is the *Dalet*. The word *Dalet* means poor and impoverished. As we have mentioned, Hebrew is read from right to left, and so, this combination of letters, the גּ and the דּ - signifies that the giver (*Gimmel*) runs after the pauper (*Dalet*) in order to contribute to him - גּ דּ. However, the poor man, in his embarrassment, turns his back on his benefactor. (Notice the form of the *Dalet* which seems to look away from the *Gimmel*.) According to mystical tradition, this giver/receiver relationship is built into the system of reality. It is also implicit in the letters and words of the Holy Language, so that by examining the word *Gimmel*, we can more fully comprehend the nature of giving. When we spell out the word *Gimmel* in Hebrew - גּמל - the word comprises two additional meanings that are necessary to appreciate this concept. In Hebrew, the vowels are separate notations placed below the letters and without the added vowels words can be read slightly altered to provide supplementary meanings. Besides giver, *Gimmel*, גּמל also means camel, *gammel* and to wean, *hegammel*. But how can camels and weaning have anything to do with the notion of giving?

According to everything we have said above, the connection is simple. Ultimate giving is bestowing goodness on another while allowing him or her to be the master and owner of that goodness. A mother who forces her 40-year-old son to wear a sweater to his wedding is not maximizing benevolence to her offspring. She is maintaining a dependent relationship with her child. The mother who can successfully wean her offspring to be independent adults is providing the essential foundation for their future. She is the *true* giver.

Similarly, the camel epitomizes independence because a camel can stock up on its water supply and then trek unassisted through a desert where life can normally not be sustained. When we empower a recipient to develop that kind of independence we have truly mastered the giving process and the recipient's pleasure is immensely enhanced.

Defining Ultimate Pleasure

We have now established that the ultimate experience of pleasure requires that you earn it. But how does wading through the world's difficulties entitle you to earn pleasure? And why is this called ultimate pleasure?

There is a counseling technique in the school of Neuro-Linguistic Programming called "core transformation." The process starts by asking the client what he or she wants and desires. In the opening stage, the client may respond that he just wants his boss to get off his back. The client's vision is narrowly focused on his immediate surroundings. "Okay," we say, "let's assume you've got that. Now what do you want?" Here the client begins to think in grander terms and may say something like, "I want wealth or fame." We again respond, "Okay, you've got that too. Now what do you want?" Inevitably, at some point in this process, the client comes up with answers like, "I want love, meaning, unity, connection, or oneness."

Now, let's be judgmental for the moment and assess whether all desires are equal. Are some desires objectively superior to others? Are some more sublime? Are others just plain inappropriate? Should a person be indulgent or ascetic? Should he or she embrace desire or flee from it?

The Talmud states that after we die, our souls are asked certain questions regarding how we lived our lives. Among those questions is a startling query: "Have you seen this beautiful world and tasted its delicious fruits?" This would seem to indicate that we should unabashedly pursue desire, yet we may think that a true spiritual life puts restrictions on pleasure seeking. So first we must understand the difference between the various types of pleasures.

Rabbi Karmi Ingber

The Relationship between Physical and Spiritual Pleasures

Let us say that a certain Mr. Smith tremendously loves hamburgers. Let's also assume that Mr. Smith has a son who is causing him a lot of difficulty and pain. If we were to say to him, "Mr. Smith, on the one hand, you love hamburgers very much, while on the other hand, your son is causing you much grief. We will trade you a lifetime's supply of hamburgers for your son." What do we imagine his response would be? What would be the response of any normal human being?

"Of course not!" he would say. The love of a child is not just greater quantitatively; it is qualitatively in a completely different dimension. In fact, the two concepts are not even comparable.

By definition, spiritual pleasures will always be much greater than physical pleasures. Physical pleasures are limited by the constraints of the physical dimension; they are based on a constant cycle of need and satiation. So, for example, if we are hungry and feel a lack, we can satisfy ourselves with a delicious meal. Afterwards, our desire for food is fulfilled and we must wait for the cycle of hunger and appeasement to start again. If we were offered the greatest delicacies in the world while we were still so full, this would be of no value to us because we presently have no lack. Mr. Smith's enjoyment of hamburgers is a pleasure, like all physical pleasures, that is limited.

Spiritual, non-tangible pleasures, on the other hand, are unbound by the physical dimension. We can never love too much. There is always the capacity for more, allowing the spiritual pleasures to grow endlessly.

The proper path is therefore to use the physical stimulation as a catapult to allow us to experience the spiritual dimension more fully. All the various aspects of our being must be accommodated appropriately. Sometimes we may need to have a really delicious meal to keep our body and emotions positive, but a person must navigate successfully not to get caught in the quagmire of only physical pleasures.

A simple but deep observation is that the most basic functions of living organisms - ingestion and reproduction - are specifically the most pleasurable. Our Sages observe that this system did not need to be constructed this way. People could eat and procreate for functional reasons even if they were not incredibly pleasurable. Yet that is precisely the point. The potentially most spiritual acts of connecting to the highest Source through creating and maintaining life can also be the most physically pleasurable! This demonstrates how the system is a single construct and physical enjoyment, when used in the higher sphere, is noble.

Conversely, to separate the physical from its spiritual root is an act of denigration. Reproduction and eating done without emotion, love and purpose, are acts that are not unique to humankind, they exist in the animal world that acts instinctively. The Torah blueprint specifically guides us through the maze of how, and in what measure, to use physical pleasures in order to avoid their pitfalls and access their power.

Additionally, without the blueprint, it is impossible to ascertain exactly which pleasures can be used as stepping stones to higher spiritual pleasures and which cannot. We can all recognize that some things are potentially very negative even if they are pleasurable. Unless we know the exact relationship between the physical and spiritual dimensions, we can never get it precisely right. That is why so many religions seek enlightenment by rejecting physical pleasures. They plainly realize that spiritual and physical pursuits generally run counter to each other, so they believe that the best approach is to abstain from the physical world. In a certain sense they are correct: without a map to navigate these dangerous waters, we are actually in grave danger.

We are fortunate that the Torah gives us the map that clearly illustrates the physical and spiritual connection. This map allows us to access, enjoy and elevate the physical world in order to experience the higher spiritual dimension. These physical actions are called the *mitzvot* of the Torah. The word *mitzvot* is generally translated as *commandments*, but there is a deeper meaning. The word *mitzvot* is rooted in the word *tzvaot* which means *connections*. The commandments of the Torah are the connecting points between the physical and spiritual dimensions. They are, so to speak, the pressure points of reality. They allow us to do an act in the physical world which affects the highest spiritual dimension, while simultaneously giving us the framework to properly navigate the physical world and its pleasures. The Torah also informs us which actions are negative, counterproductive, and can never be used as a stepping stone to a higher level.

This can be demonstrated by analyzing the Hebrew word for permissible things, *mutar*, as well as the word for forbidden things, *assur*. The literal translation of the word *mutar* is "untied," and the word *assur* means "tied" or "bound." Jewish mystics reveal that every item in the world has potentiality and can be used in some way to rectify the universe. This potential is referred to by the mystics as *netzozot hakedushah*, holy sparks, which are the actual energy packets that keep the entity in existence. When we say a certain act is *mutar*, permissible - or more correctly - untied, we are saying that the sparks of holiness in that item (or act) are free and accessible. We can perform that act, eat that food, or make that statement because its potential can be harnessed and used. When we say that something is *assur*, forbidden, or more accurately - tied up, the sparks enlivening that item at present cannot be accessed. At this time and place we do not have the ability to use that object for the betterment of the world or ourselves.

We see that permissible desires in the right dosage can be like rungs on a ladder. However, atop that ladder are even greater desires, things that we call love, unity or oneness. The mystics explain that these phrases are really just different names for the Divine, the Source of Oneness.

Ask yourself if you have ever had a time in your life that you could call a "transcendental moment." Maybe you experienced it at the birth of a child, after climbing a mountain, or in a connective instant of prayer or meditation. Now imagine multiplying that feeling by a thousand... then by a million... then by infinity. That is the closest, in our limited realm, that we can describe "experiencing the Divine." The great joys of love, unity and oneness are reflections of the Infinite Divine. Experiencing the Divine is actually experiencing the ultimate and maximum pleasure.

Review

Let's take a moment and review what we have said so far.

A) The purpose of creation is that the Benevolent Source wants to impart the greatest pleasure possible on a created entity, and that entity is humanity.

B) Ultimate pleasure is to actually experience that Perfect Being Who is the Source of all goodness and pleasure.

C) For the pleasure to be complete it needs to be earned.

Choosing Correctly (Not an Arbitrary Reward)

This brings us to the final point. The earning of the pleasure of connection to the Divine by successfully choosing between right and wrong in this complex world is not about getting rewarded for being a "good boy or girl."

Rather, we are able to experience that connection because by acting righteously we are actually becoming like God! The Eternal One is the only entity that is intrinsically perfect yet we can emulate God's perfection by perfecting ourselves through our acts of free-will. As the Eternal One gives selflessly, lovingly, and elevates the lowly, so too, we are bidden to give, help support and improve the lot of others. In this way we rectify this universe and elevate our own beings.

This concept can be demonstrated through our most basic interactions. For example, when we meet someone, the first thing we do is ask their name, where they are from or what they do. Then if we stumble onto a conversation piece, we jump on it. "Oh, you're from Connecticut! I have some friends that went to school there," etc. What we are actually doing is looking for commonality so that we can connect. Similarly, the only way to experience the Divine is to be like the Divine!

This also can explain why this world is so darn hard. If you were earning $10 a day, you wouldn't need to work so hard, but earning $1 million a day requires tremendous effort. By successfully choosing the proper path of good deeds, *mitzvot*, connectors, amid a labyrinth of confusion, we are building ultimate connection to God by becoming God-like.

This is analogous to a person who develops a taste for fine wine. As he sensitizes himself to the proper taste, he has the ability to enjoy and appreciate a really good wine while someone who does not develop that sensitivity has no appreciation for it at all.

The sensitivity we create in our lifetime is discussed by the mystics in numerous ways. Let us examine this through understanding *Kaf Hakela,* one of the possible states that can occur to a person after death. In a practical sense, *Kaf Hakela* means that after death a person becomes stuck in the consciousness one has created for oneself in this world.

Let's suppose a person spends all his time exercising his physical body. He does not concern himself with moral and ethical issues. All he thinks about the entire day is "pumping iron." When such a person's soul leaves this world, he takes that consciousness with him. He still desires to physically work out. He looks for a gym and for ways to "pump iron," but his deeper self is tortured by the fact that he has no body with which to fulfill his aspirations. On the other hand, a person who has spent his life enveloped in spiritual pursuits continues to experience the eternal spiritual dimension when he leaves this world and enters the completely spiritual realm.

We have said that in this world we actually build our connection to eternity and our experience of that pleasure. Does that mean that Judaism is a "next world" religion? Is the whole focus on the afterlife?

The answer to that question is the same as all good Jewish answers: yes, and no! In one sense, this world is the time of work. The challenges of this world and the free-will we are given to make choices in this world are the necessary components that enable us to earn our reward. The next dimension, the afterlife, is the time when truth is revealed and the ability to earn our reward has finished. The reality of the next world is solely for enjoying the fruits of our labor in this world. The Sages express the paradox with this adage: "One moment of pleasure in the next dimension is greater than all the pleasures of this world put together, yet one moment in this world, where you can earn your place through your own actions, is better than all the pleasures of the next world."

The two states serve two different primary functions. One is a time of preparation and the other a time of recompense. However, there is one important caveat we need to realize: although there isn't a guarantee that we will receive physical rewards in this world, those who live their lives properly still have a *tremendous, serene pleasure by feeling connected to the Source of existence and living their lives accordingly.* We all see how living without the appropriate boundaries actually brings disaster and unhappiness, while a true framework leads to healthy living and happiness.

Yet there is an even deeper concept here that the mystics reveal to us. These positive actions, *mitzvot* or connectors, are actually the source of pleasure themselves! Since they connect us to the ultimate Source, these actions themselves bring happiness. This is the deeper meaning of the idea that living a righteous life makes us joyful and fulfilled. Doing so actually connects us to what is good and pleasurable. The difference is that in this world of "work," we are only able to sense the connection partially; while in the dimension of "recompense," we experience the connection fully!

Connecting the Dots

Now let's revisit the idea we discussed earlier, that before a soul comes into this world, it is basking in the Supernal Light, but needs to come into this world to earn its connection to that Light. The great Sage, the Chofetz Chaim, gives an illuminating parable to this process. He tells a story about a man named Yankel who lived in a town in Europe. Yankel and his family were very poor, and Yankel strived for ways to improve their lot. One day he heard a tale of a distant place, where there were supposedly jewels, gold and silver lying on the streets, easily accessible and there for the taking.

The journey to this land was long and treacherous. There was only one boat a year that traveled there and the trip itself took an entire year. Yankel understood that he would be away from his beloved family for at least three years, with the traveling there and back, and one year working until the next boat set sail again. It was a heavy price to pay, but well worth the potential gain. Yankel informed his wife and children that he was determined to make the trip in the hopes of changing their fate forever.

He made the journey and when he arrived on the shores, to his surprised delight, Yankel saw that all the tales he heard were true. There were rubies, diamonds and sapphires lying in the streets. Everywhere he turned there was an abundance of precious gems. Yankel quickly scooped up all he could hold, when suddenly a local man approached him and said, "What's your big rush, friend?"

Yankel answered him and the man continued, "You have your priorities upside down. If you are here for at least one full year, you need to know that in this country, we don't give a hoot about jewels and gold. We have tons of that stuff. What's precious here is something completely different. You see, there is very little daylight in this region, so what is valuable here are things that are flammable. If you focus your time on gathering oils, fats and shortening, you will be a rich man; otherwise, you will be worthless in these parts."

Yankel listened to this local. He believed his logic and started the process of gathering fats, oils and shortenings to sell. Eventually Yankel gathered a huge supply of these oils, and he becomes a wealthy merchant in this country, opening a chain of stores called *Yankel's Shmaltz Shortening Supplies.* And so life continued and he was considered very successful.

One day Yankel was startled by the sound of a powerful whistle blow. "What is that?" he wondered, when suddenly he realized what it was and the impact of the whistle blowing was like a wake-up call. He felt like he was hit by a policeman's billy club.

"That is the sound of the boat that is sailing back to Europe!" he realized in shock. "I have to get back quickly! The boat is about to sail!" So Yankel hurriedly gathered all the wealth he had amassed that year, his treasure chests of oils and fats, and he lugged them to the docks. As he got closer to the boat, he remembered that he came all this way for something entirely different. He looked longingly at the streets paved with jewels and remembered that he came to bring home some of these precious gems!

The boat's whistle was now a frantic cry to him that there was no time left! The captain called out, "Everyone aboard!"

Yankel was paralyzed. He hastily grabbed a diamond in the road, stuck it in his coat pocket and loaded the boat with his fat supplies.

After a few days at sea, there was a terrible stench. The crew determined that Yankel's treasure chests were the source of the problem. They pried open the containers of fats and the horrid stench wafted throughout the boat. The oils and fats had all gone rancid. The captain ordered everything to be thrown overboard. And so went all of Yankel's "wealth"!

When Yankel finally arrived home, his wife eagerly greeted him, anxious to see the vast wealth he had brought home to them. But Yankel's response was simply, "I don't want to talk about it." He went home and slept for days. His concerned wife started rummaging through his things and found in the pocket of Yankel's coat the diamond he grabbed before leaving.

She rushed off to have it appraised. When she returned, she woke up her husband ecstatically. "We are rich!" she exclaimed. "You are a genius!"

"No," he sadly responded, "you don't understand. There were jewels everywhere. I could have gathered so much more, but I forgot what I went for."

The Chofetz Chaim's parable describes the soul that descends to this world, the world of darkness, where truth is concealed. The soul needs to come into this darkened dimension to choose correctly in order to earn its pleasure. In this world there are jewels throughout the streets. These are the opportunities to do spiritual and moral acts, the *mitzvot*. At every turn we can find opportunities that bring true wealth and eternal connection. This is what we came here for in the first place.

Unfortunately, we often forget to gather the truly valuable jewels that will have worth after we leave this world. We get caught up in gathering temporal things of no real significance. The fats and oils are the currencies that are valued in this world, the fame and wealth, which turns rancid and is worthless when we leave this world. And although we may grab a diamond or two in passing, once we understand that the whole purpose of our being in this world is to gain the ultimate pleasure through choosing and living appropriately, we will want to maximize our time and never forget to gather the true, precious jewels that life offers us. (4*)

Summary:

1. The purpose of creation is to give a created being ultimate pleasure.

2. The ultimate pleasure is experiencing the Eternal Source.

3. The greatest experience of God is when we earn that experience by becoming similar to God.

4. Choosing righteously in this world is the means to become similar to God and earn ultimate pleasure.

5. This world is essentially designed for work, i.e., a means to the end.

THE PRACTICAL APPLICATION:

After we have understood the system, we need to find ways to put the lessons into practice. In this section, we will share some hands-on activities to help make the concepts we have discussed feel real to us. We can work on them one at a time, taking as many days as we need to repeat the themes and methods, until they are part of our psyche.

Afterwards, try the next practical application exercise. Only do the practical work after you have finished the appropriate chapter on the theory, so that your acquired knowledge can allow you to be more creative and expansive in your approach.

Application One:

Let's see how knowing the purpose of our existence can change and enhance our lives.

First, meditate on the idea that everything that is happening in our lives is a means and an opportunity for us to respond appropriately. This whole world is a testing ground and we have the ability to succeed by making worthwhile decisions.

Focus on the fact that our existence is meaningful and we are earning eternity through dealing with our challenges.

Concentrate on the idea that according to what we now know, true success is making correct moral decisions and living spiritually. For example, if a business competitor speaks negatively about us and it is very painful, try to remember that our moral and appropriate response is what we are being judged on.

So instead of focusing on how this negativity may lower our status in the business world, we can do one positive action in response: we can control our anger, we can consciously decide not to stoop to his or her low level (even while setting the record straight). We can revel in the fact that we are earning eternity by doing this positive act and contrast that to what we thought we had lost.

This is done by realizing that **our goal (*the pleasure that will be fully experienced through living properly*) and our means (*the acts of living properly*) are so much more valuable than the difficulty of the challenge.** This is called "keeping your eye on the ball."

Tell yourself throughout the day, "The righteous acts I do are why I am alive."

Carefully perform one such action a day with that thought in mind. Revel in the joy of that knowledge.

Repeat to yourself the following adage: My purpose is to live righteously. I'm doing **this act** to help accomplish that.

Application Two:

Prioritize your life. Concentrate on the different things we want in life. Think about how much time we are occupied with physical pleasures. Compare that with the time and effort we are investing in pursuing spiritual and non-tangible gratification. Compare the satisfaction we receive from each type of pleasure.

Now, expound upon the spiritual pleasures: Imagine love and oneness in the grandest terms and emotions you can muster. Try to remember a time of connectedness, a transcendental moment. If you cannot remember any such time in your life, create it now. Close off your mind to all extraneous thoughts and focus on the Endless Source of all life.

We can accomplish this through many ways. Here are some suggestions:

Repeat a phrase that will focus you on this reality. For example, you can repeat the phrase: "***Ein Od Milvado*** -There is no other"- until your mind is connected to a deeper reality.

If you are more visual, you can focus on a Divine Name of God and etch it into your mind's eye until you are enveloped with that concept alone.

For the more down to earth types: begin to speak freely to the Creator, the Source of all life. Speak about your difficulties. Ask for assistance. Freely associate in this state of dialogue until you feel connected.

After you have completed this exercise, **imagine multiplying this transcendental spiritual feeling manifold.** Recognize the hierarchy of pleasures and do something that is rewarding in a more spiritual way. For example, actively pursue doing an act of kindness. Express love to your spouse and family members, friends or neighbors, through a benevolent deed. Fan the fire of those emotions until you appreciate the joys of the spiritual dimension.

Repeat the adage: *These values I am creating will last with me for eternity.*

Application Three:

Unite your system of pleasures, allowing them to work like rungs in a ladder leading you higher. Remember that there is a place for physical pleasures, but they need to be a catapult to help us grow and experience the higher dimensions. Now, let's make this real. Take a raisin or some other delicious fruit in your right hand (if you are a lefty, hold it in your left). We are about to experience the interconnectedness of all pleasure to the Source of the pleasure. As the Sages tell us, when you prepare yourself appropriately for the pleasure, the experience is that much greater. While holding the raisin in your hand, say the following blessing slowly, clearly enunciating and focusing on every word which will connect you to the Source of the pleasure:

"Baruch Atah Ado-noi Elo-heinu Melech HaOlam Borei pri ha'aitz." (The Source of all blessing is You, God, Master of the universe, Who creates the fruit of the tree.)

Now, with your eyes closed, slowly chew the raisin and allow every burst of flavor to encircle your mouth. Keep chewing the fruit and enjoying every iota of its delights, appreciating that this was created by the Master of All to give us pleasure to be content and joyous and accomplish great things. Leisurely continue chewing for a long while with a sense of gratitude and awe. We are now connecting our lower and higher aspects as an integrated whole. We can continue to do the same thing with all *mutar* (permissible) pleasures.

Endnotes

(1*) *One can argue that just as God could have made us in a way that we don't need to feel pain to know pleasure, He could have also built us in a way that we don't care if we "earn it" or not. However, in truth, the need to feel like we "earned it" is not simply an emotional state, rather it is a reflection of the form of a human being (Tzuras HaAdam). A human being wants to earn things because we are actually an entity that affects reality and thereby does earn things. To make us feel like we don't need to earn something when in actuality we are built with the ability and mission to affect change, would be to alter the actual content of the human being and have us live in an illusion. Similarly, although we have presented at this point in the text the idea that pleasure can be perceived without pain, later we will present the perspective that it is fundamental for humankind to be built in a way where we know something by rejecting it's opposite. Accordingly, the fleeing from evil does lead to attaining good, awareness of the negative does enhance understanding the good, and knowing pain does facilitate pleasure.*

(2*) *It is mistakenly assumed that the Hebrew alphabet was derived from the Greeks. We see that the opposite is actually true; the Greek alphabet is rooted in the Hebrew. This is evidenced by the fact that all the names for the Hebrew letters have meaning, as we have discussed above, while the Greek Alpha (Hebrew Aleph), Beta (Hebrew Bet), Gamma (Hebrew Gimmel) and Delta (Hebrew Dalet), etc., all have no literal meaning. Additionally, the Greek language has a numerical system as does the Hebrew language, yet when we go through the normal order of the Greek* *alphabet with Alpha having the numerical value 1 and Beta having the numerical value 2, etc., the number 6 is conspicuously missing. The fifth letter Epsilon is 5, but the sixth letter Zeta is numerically valued as 7! This is because the Greek pronunciation did not include the Hebrew sound for the sixth letter "Vav"; the Greeks therefore skipped that letter, but remained true to the Hebrew numerical system and gave their sixth letter Zeta the numerical value of 7. As opposed to the Hebrew in which the sixth letter Vav is 6 and the seventh letter Zayin (in Greek Zeta) is 7.*

(3*) For example, the ancient Hebrew words for truth and falsehood are Emet, אמת, *and Sheker,* שקר. *Each of the Hebrew letters in the word Emet, stand on 'two feet.' The Hebrew letters of the word Sheker precariously stand on 'one foot'. This signifies that Truth is solid, grounded and lasting while Falsehood teeters on no foundation and cannot last.*

The letters of the word Emet are also the first, middle and last letters of the Hebrew alphabet. This signifies that truth must be consistent throughout, from the beginning to the end, symbolized by the fact that the letters are the first, the middle and the end.

Moreover, we can't play around with truth. This is evident from the fact that if we take away the first letter from the word Emet, the letter Alef, the letters that remain, מת, *spell the word 'meit', which means dead. Altering truth even slightly is akin to death.*

Alternatively, the Hebrew letter Alef, by virtue of the fact that its numerical value is one and is the only letter in the language that has no actual sound, means that it represents the Ineffable; the Godliness and spirituality in the world. The word Alef itself means the Supreme One – the Alufo shel olam– the Master of the world. If we take out the spiritual life force from the truth, we are surely left with death and decay.

In addition, there are many variations of Gematria, Jewish numerology, and one system is called Dimished Gematria (gematria Ketanah) which consists of removing all values of tens or hundreds to bring the word to its lowest basic components. When we do this with the word Emet, the Diminished Gematria of truth is the number nine. Some refer to nine as the number of truth because no matter how we combine it, it remains nine:

9 x 1 = 9, 9 x 2 = 18, 18 is itself 1 + 8 which equals 9, 9 x 3 = 27, 27 is 2 + 7 = 9, 9 x 4 = 36, etc. This peculiarity of the number nine works in many other mathematical formulas and calculations which indicates some aspect of truth embedded in the number which is reflected in the word for truth, Emet.

The letters of the word Sheker, however, are consecutive letters of the Hebrew alphabet, but that they are out of order. This represents the idea that lies are "close together", there can be many different false answers to any question while truth is not commonly found.

There are 27 letters in the Hebrew alphabet, including the five "double" letters. If we count the letters of the Hebrew alphabet, between the first letter of the word Emet, א, to the middle letter, מ, and from the middle letter to the last letter, ת, we find 13 letters. Counting up the numerical value of the word for "one"- echad - אחד equals 13: 4 = ד + 8 = ח + 1 = א = 13). This means there is one truth built into the word Emet, while potential lies are numerous.

Not only can we elaborate much more on just these words Emet and Sheker, but the amazing thing is that this can be done with every Hebrew word! As the Mystics teach us, the secrets of the universe and the formation of reality itself is contained in the Holy tongue.

(4*) To elaborate further: We have defined our higher aspect as being in search of spiritual pleasures. However, there is an even greater level which we strive for and that is the level where we do what is right because it is right, and not for reward. There is a story told about the great Sage, the Gaon of Vilna, who was not able to find a lulav and etrog in his freezing Lithuanian town. (The lulav and etrog are two of the species used for the mitzvah of shaking the lulav and etrog during Sukkot, the festival of Tabernacles.) In hopes of helping him, his attendants searched until they found a Jew who had a beautiful lulav and etrog. Of course they tried to buy them for the Gaon's use.

But this man refused to sell them for even exorbitant amounts of money. Finally, he made the following offer. "I know that the intention of the Gaon while doing this mitzvah will be much greater than anything I could muster. I will give these items to him to do the mitzvah on one condition – that all the reward he receives for this act is transferred to me."

To the surprise of his disciples, the Gaon did not hesitate a moment and quickly agreed to the deal. And they wanted to understand why he was willing to relinquish his reward for this mitzvah. He then explained that this was a moment of tremendous joy for him because all his life he was concerned that the altruism of his deeds would be compromised because he knew that one day he would be rewarded for all his actions.

"Finally I was given the opportunity to do a mitzvah for completely selfless and noble reasons, just for the love of the Creator, with no thought of reward!"

CHAPTER TWO

FATE AND DESTINY

....

Now that we understand that our purpose is actualized by the decisions we make in this life, does that mean we all decide the same thing? Isn't everyone's situation unique and, consequently, aren't different approaches required? Can people really choose "correctly" when their situations often seem to be prearranged? To understand this, we must investigate the depths of what we call "Fate and Destiny" ...

Are we really free to create our destiny or is life predetermined?

This is an age-old philosophical question, dealt with by many cultures. The answer will greatly impact our lives. If our lives are predetermined, in the classic sense of the word, there is nothing we can do to change our destinies. Our whole life is simply going through the motions, feeling as if we are making decisions when, in fact, everything has already been decided. Whether we will succeed in business, or even which business we will choose, has already been preordained: the same with our health, sickness, wealth or poverty. Whether we will meet with a secret lover and cheat on our spouse or stay faithful: it's all written and engraved somewhere in the heavens.

The Greek Concept of Fate

What exactly do we mean when we say, "It was meant to be"? Who meant it to be and why? And if "that" was meant to be, how come we take credit for our brilliant business or social acumen? Wasn't that also meant to be? Many people think of a certain incident or situation as their "fate." The word *fate* is actually a Greek term, referring to the three goddesses called the Fates. One spins out the thread of life, one apportions the length of the yarn, and one cuts the thread. The ancient Greeks believed that all good and evil that befalls a person is unalterably woven into his or her destiny by these Fates. This concept is articulated in the classic Greek tale of Oedipus.

Oedipus was born to the King and Queen of Thebes. His parents were warned by the Oracle that Oedipus is destined to kill his father King Laius, so baby Oedipus is given to a herdsman to be killed. The herdsman has pity on him and eventually he is brought to the King and Queen of Corinth who adopt him and raise him as their son. When Oedipus grows up, he is informed by the Oracle that he is destined to kill his father and marry his mother. In a desperate attempt to evade his fate, Oedipus flees from Corinth to Thebes. On the road to Thebes, Oedipus has an altercation with a man and kills him. Unbeknownst to Oedipus, the man he slays is none other than his biological father, King Laius of Thebes. Afterwards, Oedipus continues on his journey. Through his wit, he is able to destroy the Sphinx monster. This earns him the reward of marrying the recently widowed Queen of Thebes, who, of course, is none other than his biological mother.

And so the first neurosis is born.

Oedipus's fate has caught up with him. As decreed, he has killed his father and married his mother. When a terrible drought strikes, Oedipus consults the Oracle and is told that the drought is a result of his actions. Confronted with the truth, Oedipus blinds and exiles himself, his mother hangs herself and, as in every great Greek tragedy, "they all live happily ever after." In any case, this classic tale exemplifies the Greek notion of fate.

Many concepts of the ancient Greeks were vehemently opposed by the Sages of Israel and this doctrine of predetermination is no exception. The Sages explained that man is certainly free to choose. In fact, without freedom of choice, life would be meaningless and the purpose of creation nonsensical.

Freedom of Choice in the Face of Limitations

Yet if we think through the issue honestly, we will see that it's not so simple. We can ask ourselves: How free am I really? Did I determine who my parents would be, or which era I was born into, or how I would look or even which type of personality I have?

There is an old argument in psychology about what forms personality: is it nature or nurture? I maintain that this is a dilemma if a person only has one child. Anyone who has more than one child will see the different tendencies almost immediately. I remember one of my children was so cuddly and affectionate; she was content to always be snuggling with her mother. Another child showed fierce independence from day one. If I could put words in her mouth, I knew exactly what this second child would have said. Any time we were taking care of her, she stared at us defiantly, as if to assert, "I will change my own diaper, thank you very much!" Clearly, there are innate predispositions from the outset of life and, of course, how we nurture those tendencies affects the person each one becomes. Still it seems to be that we are working within a somewhat preordained system.

What about the events that occur to us from outside of ourselves? Are those predetermined?

Obviously, we see that a person can affect his longevity through making bad choices. A person is free to jump off a skyscraper and, in all likelihood, abruptly end his existence. Or he can abuse his body for a long time and may eventually die of disease. But let's put all that aside for the moment and ask: Is there a preordained time limit on the length of each of our lives?

Some people seem to break every rule of healthy living and live to ripe old ages, while others become obsessed with every health fad and still drop dead in their prime. How about wealth and poverty? Sometimes we see people who are lazy and not too bright strike gold on every business decision they make, while smarter, more industrious people can't succeed on the simplest monetary deals. Certainly it seems that many areas of our lives are "prearranged," but if that is true, what happens to the Sages' tenet that we have free-will?

Let us start with an area in which we have complete and utter freedom: that place is within our heads.

In our minds, we are free to decide upon anything we want. A human being's existence is divided into three components: our thoughts, our speech and our actions. Generally speaking, on the thought level, we are totally free to make whatever decisions we want.

The next level is the speech dimension, and although usually what we decide to say is what ends up coming out, occasionally something else slips out of our mouths. Similarly, our decision to do a certain action usually comes to fruition, but sometimes that action is thwarted for some reason or another. This happens in the action realm more frequently than in the speech dimension. So, for example, we may decide to give charity to a pauper and reach our hand into our pocket to pull out some coins. As we stretch our hand out to do this act of kindness, the coins slip from our hand and fall down the sewer. Our free-will decision was to give charity, but the action was not brought into reality. On a simple level, this may just be because we are clumsy. But on a deeper level, there may be greater forces at play and it is possible that we were "prevented" from giving the charity. There's a myriad of possible rationales why our intention was not achieved. To get a picture of how complex this can be, imagine our beggar was a recovered drug addict and had decided to return to his former habit with our donation. As he sees his cash for the drugs dropping down the drain, a thought enters his mind: "Was losing the money a sign that I shouldn't go back to my old ways?"

At this point, you may protest, "What are you saying here? If the action I want to take is *prevented* by some other force, how do I have free-will?" The answer is that we are actually judged on the fortitude of our decision to perform an act. If we wanted to do something good (1*) and for some overriding reason it didn't come to be, according to Jewish tradition, we are generally credited as if we have performed the intended act! It is now up to the Omniscient One to calculate how and if that act should affect the world.

This freedom in our minds - our freedom of thought - cannot be overstated. We often make ourselves victims to our situation and do not appreciate the level of control that we have. Most of us fall prey to this problem which starts early in our training. How many times have you heard a child explain why he hit his friend or sibling with the words, "He made me do it"? Whenever my kids would use that excuse, I would question them. "What exactly do you mean, *he made me do it*? Did he take your hand and smash it against his own body?" "No, he just got me so mad," the child protests. I then reframe the statement to my child. "So if I understand correctly, you let *yourself* get angry and then felt like hitting your sibling. If so, let me share with you the famous story of the great Sage Hillel and how he was able to master his responses."

Hillel was a beloved Sage in Israel in ancient times, "the Prince" of the Sanhedrin. He was renowned for his humility and piety, and greatly beloved by the Jewish people. One day two jokers were talking and one dared his friend, "I'll bet you that even with all your crazy antics, you can't get Hillel angry." His buddy was intrigued by the challenge and said, "You got yourself a bet." And so, the two jokers wagered four hundred gold coins to see if one of them could anger Hillel. The troublemaker waited for the opportune moment, which was definitely on Friday afternoon. On Friday afternoon, when everyone in Jerusalem is hurrying to prepare for the Sabbath, the troublemaker was sure that under such pressure, Hillel could be made to pop.

As the Sabbath approached and Hillel hurried to the bathhouse to prepare himself for the holy day, he heard someone scream his name throughout the street of Jerusalem. "Hillel! Where is Hillel?" the troublemaker demanded. Hillel had just finished disrobing but he redressed and went outside to see what the ruckus was about and why he was needed.

The troublemaker challenged him, "Are you Hillel?"

"Yes I am. How can I help you my son?"

"Tell me," the troublemaker demanded, "why do you Babylonians have such funny shaped heads?"

Now, Hillel was from Babylonia, and it was an insulting question. "That is a great question," Hillel responded and he proceeded to seriously answer the joker's question.

When he finished, Hillel re-entered the bathhouse and the same thing happened again. He heard his name called throughout the streets of Jerusalem. Again, he redressed and went out, and was presented with another bizarre and irrelevant question.

Hillel answered without flinching. When the troublemaker started his antics a third time, Hillel said again, "How can I help you my son?"

"Oh, I have so many questions, but I'm afraid maybe you'll get upset with me."

"Ask all your questions," Hillel patiently assured him.

"Are you Hillel the one they say is the Prince of Israel?"

"Yes, son," Hillel replied.

"Well, if that is true, there should be no more like you!"

"Why is that, my son?"

"Because I just lost four hundred gold coins because of you!"

Hillel smiled and explained to him, "You lost four hundred and you may lose another four hundred, but you will never, ever get Hillel angry!"

What an outrageous statement! How can anyone guarantee that it is impossible for him to get mad? Hillel felt comfortable making that guarantee because he had complete control over his free-will responses. He was the master of his thoughts and no one could dictate his reactions. In this place, he was completely free.

After hearing this story so many times, my children slowly grew to hate it. They hesitated to fight with their siblings because they knew that if they did, the dreaded Hillel story was not far behind. "Okay," I announced whenever I heard a fight brewing, "did I ever tell you kids the story of how nobody could get Hillel angry for all the money in the world?"

"No, Daddy!" they begged. "Not the Hillel story again! We'll stop fighting! Just please not that story another time!"

On one level, it can be intimidating to realize our complete responsibility for our actions and reactions, but on a deeper level, it is quite freeing for us to recognize the tremendous power we have been given over ourselves.

We Are Not "Fated" Even When Circumstances Are Prearranged

Now you may be wondering if I have just pulled a fast one on you. We have discussed man's great freedom, especially in decisions of the mind; but didn't we demonstrate earlier that man is actually not so free? Didn't we say that one is obviously born with certain constraints and didn't we posit that certain events in one's life might even be preordained? Well, if that is so, how are we free at all? Is a person who is born tone deaf able to freely decide to become a singer? Is a woman born to a poor family that can't afford schooling really free to become a brain surgeon? If someone's genetic map destines him for a short life, is he really free to change that?

Furthermore, the Talmud teaches that people are born with certain traits and that being born at specific times actually influences our predisposition. For example, a person born under the sign of *MaAdim* (Mars) is believed to be bloodthirsty. He might be one of those kids in high school biology class who is really into dissecting the frog. He thrives on agitating his squeamish peers by pulling on the creature in bizarre ways and tossing the hapless reptile about. The Sages discuss what a person born with such a temperament should do. Apparently, he is not so free, after all.

The approach of the Sages to this personality type seems to be even more confusing. They say that he should become a *shochet,* a person who ritually slaughters animals to make them kosher for eating, or a surgeon, or even a surgeon that can perform circumcisions, which would be an especially noble way to elevate this trait. So although it is possible to overcome inborn characteristics, we are advised in this case that the effort may not be worth the reward. Rather we should follow the advice of King Solomon in Proverbs, in which he writes, "Train a child according to his own unique way." So what kind of freedom do we really have here?

To understand this properly, we must define the well-known Hebrew word *mazel.* Oh, that's easy, you think to yourself, we are always wishing people a hearty "*Mazel tov*" at weddings, births and other auspicious occasions. It means "good luck." However, if we think it through, we will quickly realize that this is incorrect. Such an idea would be completely contrary to the basic tenets of Jewish belief. Jews believe that the Almighty is completely and constantly involved in our lives and nothing is arbitrary or accidental. So wishing someone "good luck" on their marriage is tantamount to giving the happy couple a rabbit's foot for a wedding gift. It's just not part of the system.

The word *mazel* comes from the term *nozel*, which literally means *what flows down*. *Mazel* is not luck at all; rather, it is what "flows" specifically to us from above. *The mazel we are given are the circumstances that flow down to us to create the framework of our life.* Our *mazel* includes our predisposition to certain traits. It even affects our longevity, our financial station and our offspring. In a certain sense, it does limit some of our choices, but that isn't the freedom of choice we are talking about. The freedom of choice we are referring to is *the ability to make moral decisions!* Our *mazel* is the tools we are given and the circumstances we may find ourselves in. But within that situation, we are completely free to choose what really counts: the choice between right and wrong, good and evil, the lofty or the loathsome.

The person who is born with an affinity for blood has a certain *mazel*, a tool that flows down to him as part of his task, but he is the one who decides if he will be a killer or a redeemer. The reason such a person is advised to become a doctor is not because traits cannot be overcome. Obviously, if a trait were objectively negative (2*), a person must be equipped with the free-will to overcome it. Otherwise it would impinge on his moral autonomy.

Rather, if someone's mazel includes a certain trait, we understand that it was given to him or her specifically to express his or her unique task. We all have our personal strengths and challenges - that is our distinct *mazel*. Our *mazel* is the *means* we are given to accomplish the ends. If one person's *mazel* is wealth, it is a test for one to be generous and not selfish and haughty. A poor man has his own individual trials and tribulations and must grapple with the danger of turning to theft or becoming an embittered person. We may all want to have the *mazel* of the wealthy, but in the grand scheme of things the greater issue is not the tools we are given, but rather how we use them to build ourselves. So when we wish someone a *Mazel Tov*, we are blessing them that the tools they have been given (their *mazel*) should be such that they will successfully use it to accomplish their goals. We are blessing them to become the greatest moral and righteous human being they can be, in their own unique, individual way. That is truly good *mazel*.

We can agree with the Greeks that Oedipus did not choose his parents, nor could he control *their* actions, but the choice to kill the stranger on the road was made with his free-will and that moral decision was completely in his hands. He was free to choose otherwise *and accordingly, everything in his life would have turned out completely different.*

Let's quickly review:

1. Certain things in life (our *mazel*) are prearranged to provide the unique set of circumstances for our own assignment.

(Note: there are other factors that affect what happens to you, most importantly the outgrowth of your positive or negative actions, as will be discussed later.)

2. We are given complete freedom to choose, especially in areas that involve ethics.

3. The choices we make help reveal our unique destiny.

Can Prearranged Circumstances (*Mazel*) Be Changed?

Now you may find the idea that we have a decreed *mazel* a bit disturbing. The fact that we have no limits on our ethical choices is only a partial solace. It still cramps our style to work within a certain framework. We may be free to choose to become psychologists, business people, police officers or anything else we want, but still, our innate tendencies do push us in certain directions. And what's even worse is the thought that our success and failure may be influenced by our *mazel*! So we are left with the question: is there a way to change our *mazel*?

The Talmud records an incident that occurred to the great Sage Rabbi Akivah. Rabbi Akivah was once informed by a certain stargazer that his daughter would die on her wedding day. Since Rabbi Akivah did not put too much stock in stargazers because he understood that God completely runs the world, he wasn't too concerned. Yet the prediction lay at the back of his mind until the actual time of his daughter's engagement. When Rabbi Akivah's daughter got married it was a tremendous celebration with all the great leaders of the generation present. After the ceremony, the new bride and groom went to their abode for the evening. The next morning, Rabbi Akivah came to visit and was shocked by what he saw. He pointed out to his daughter that there was a snake in between the stones of the wall and a large hairpin was pierced through its skull. His daughter hadn't noticed the snake at all and told her father that the evening before, when the room was pitch dark, she had removed her hairpin and stuck it in between the stones of the wall. She had inadvertently killed the snake that was mere inches from her head.

"Tell me," inquired Rabbi Akivah, "did you do anything special recently?" She reflected and hesitantly admitted that at the wedding celebration everyone was having such a great time singing and dancing that when a poor man came to the door of the hall no one heard or helped him.

"I noticed him though, and realized that he was hungry," she told her father. "I gave him my portion of food for dinner." (In those days, I guess there were no "doubles" even for the bride!) Rabbi Akivah told her that she did a great act of charity and the merit of the benevolent act helped save her life.

There are many things we learn from this strange story. We see that although Rabbi Akivah did not give the stargazers credence, he was still somewhat apprehensive, and at the end of the story, *he even admitted the validity of the prediction!* Still, his daughter's act of charity and kindness changed the outcome.

What is this business of stargazers? Is there any truth to astrology? We know to be cautious around possible charlatans in this field. However, there is something to this system when it is understood properly. We have a book in our possession whose authorship our tradition traces back to the first homo-sapiens, Adam (in Hebrew, called *Adam HaRishon*). In this book there is a diagram of the constellations and discussion of the different planetary effects. Adam's diagrams and names for the various zodiac signs are basically the same as we have today, except that, according to the solar calendar, the zodiac signs end around the 22nd of each month, while according to the Jewish lunar calendar (based on the cycles of the moon) each month has its own sign. So since we acknowledge some credibility in this system, let's try and understand how it really works.

We know that there are spiritual dimensions that the Creator established. The flow that the Creator imparts to the world passes through these spiritual dimensions or conduits until it reaches the physical world. These spiritual dimensions parallel the world we live in, in a certain way. It is as if you built an acoustically refined room and placed a large guitar in one corner and a smaller one on the other side. When you pluck the strings of the large instrument, it causes the smaller one to resonate as well. Similarly, the spiritual dimension passes the flow to the physical dimension (actually, the flow moves the other way as well, a phenomenon we will discuss later). In this way, the entire system is like a holographic image. Every world is a reflection of another world, only on different levels. The remnants and imprints of the influences that are transmitted through these dimensions can be read by those who understand the system. It is not that the planets and stars themselves have an effect on anything. Rather, since the system is like a holographic image - the parts contain the whole - the transmission can be seen in this world by one who knows how to read it. In ancient times certain individuals and nations were experts at interpreting these signs. The Talmud tells us that Abraham (in Hebrew, Avraham) was a world-renowned specialist in this field, so much so that people throughout the world sought out his services and advice.

On the one hand, Rabbi Akivah understood that the stargazer might be reading the map correctly to some degree. However, he also knew that even the experts among these people were only picking up vague imprints, so there was no reason to be overly concerned. And even more importantly, he knew that all these systems were superseded by the will of the Omnipotent Source.

In the end Rabbi Akivah saw that the stargazer had seen correctly. The *mazel* of his daughter was for her to live only a short eighteen years of life. Among the tools she was given was a brief life-span and she would be judged on how she acted during that brief time.

But if her *mazel* was for a short life, what happened?

The answer is that the tools for our mission, i.e., our unique *mazel*, are not static. Our *mazal* can be changed! So even the prearranged circumstances of your life are themselves subject to change based on your free-will decisions. The kind act of Rabbi Akivah's daughter actually altered the amount of time that she was allotted on this earth. *The stargazers are by definition incorrect because the free-will of humankind can change our circumstances.*

This was part of Avraham's own development in life. He was the first person to recognize, through the use of rational thinking, that there must be only one Omnipotent Creator. Yet he also saw that certain things were prearranged. He therefore thought that he was bound to function within those specific confines. According to the Midrash, his capacity to read the "signs" led him to believe that he would not have a child. However, through years of struggle and development, he was eventually enlightened to flee from the world of astrology and stargazing. The true Source of the emanation showed him that the flow can be changed. The Omnipotent One directs the world constantly and the choices of humankind are an integral part of that system.

Avraham was granted a new *mazel*. The Omnipotent One told him, "Avraham, leave your astrology behind. I will rearrange the stars for you." Sarah gave birth to Isaac (in Hebrew, Yitzchak) long after normal childbearing age. Indeed, this supernatural approach to life became the hallmark and the anthem of their descendants (3*). The history of the Jewish people is beyond comprehension. Natural rationalizations cannot explain how the Jewish people have survived, exist and prosper. It is engraved in the inception of the Jewish Nation that we begin where things are impossible. The existence of the Jewish people demonstrates not to believe that one is bound by any conventional limitations. As we see with Rabbi Akivah's daughter, though according to her *mazel* she shouldn't even exist, it was within her ability to change the cosmic design.

Why and How Can Mazel Change If It Is Supposed to Be Part of Your Unique Challenges?

Okay, we are getting a little more encouraged now as the potential for our freedom seems to be expanding. We sigh in relief to understand that we are not totally subjected to our *mazel*. Still, the whole idea is perplexing. Let's review for a moment. We said that we are given a certain *mazel* so that we can make our ethical choices within that framework and that those unique challenges help bring out our inner selves. But if that is so, why should we be able to change our *mazel* at all? Isn't our unique *mazel* the circumstances that we need as individuals to grow? If our *mazel* is changed, doesn't that indicate that the framework we were given initially wasn't right for us?

We can delve into this question more deeply by first understanding the circumstances that can cause one's *mazel* to change. It is obviously not spurious and arbitrary things that can alter the arranged systems of the world. Rather, changing our *mazel* can be accomplished by changing our actions (including prayer), changing our name or changing our place.

Let's start with change or improvement of actions and understand why that may rewire our *mazel*.

When I lived in Israel, one of the beautiful things I saw in our community was that when a woman gave birth, the neighbors cooked meals for the family for an entire month. (This may explain why we all had so many kids. It was definitely worth it!) So let's imagine for a moment that one of the women in the community has a unique quality that she needs to express in the world, and this is her amazing trait of kindness. Its actualization is the goal and mission of her life. Accordingly, she will be given certain tools to allow her to express this quality, including (in this example) the skills of being a gifted baker and organizer. And so this woman successfully spearheads many initiatives to assist mothers after birth. Her *mazel* in terms of finances, however, is meager and she can only afford the smallest of ovens. It is a great challenge for her to keep giving to the community when she is constantly trying to juggle all the cakes in such a small space. Now, since the purpose of her *mazel* is to bring to fruition her aspect of kindness, it is possible that the Almighty may decide to give her new "tools" and new "means" to accomplish these ends. Her financial situation may change for the better, thereby providing her with better resources to accomplish her goal. **Her positive acts are themselves, in fact, the catalyst for the change.** Since she has used her meager *mazel* fully to accomplish her task, she may now deserve a better *mazel* to do even more!

But here's the hitch: After being granted new financial resources, she has a new and greater challenge on her hands. She can decide to give up all that hassle of baking for people and focus on her own pleasures. She may think that she is now a wealthy woman so why should she bother with such mundane hassles? Or she can buy herself a giant oven and express her kindness in an even greater way! Or maybe she will decide to use her baking and organizational skills to create a company that will help mothers after birth and anyone else in need. **In the same way, our destiny doesn't change, but the tools we are given to realize that destiny can change dramatically.**

Similarly, changing one's name can affect one's *mazel*. There is an ancient Jewish practice to add or change the name of a person who has become seriously ill. How does that possibly help? It sounds almost superstitious to believe that changing a name will change a person's fortune.

However, changing a name is based on the concept that our name represents the essence of the person (4*) and when we change our name, we are taking upon ourselves a change in our actual being. We are declaring that we are different now and therefore we are entitled to a different *mazel*. Of course, the name change must be accompanied by real personal change. In the case of adding a name to a young child or infant who is not old enough to do things differently, usually the name "Chaya" or "Chaim" which mean "life" or "Raphael" which means "God heals" is added as a way to add the *mazel* of healing and life.

Finally, a change of place can change one's *mazel*. How does this work? Is this not just running away from one's situation?

Here is an example that may shed some light on this strange concept.

Imagine there is a guy from Europe named Yankel. (As you may notice, all of my European Jews are named Yankel.) Yankel's destiny is to help build education and knowledge in the world. But Yankel lives in Poland and he is dirt poor. He works in a very common field for the impoverished Jews of Europe: Yankel is a Cheder Rebbe, a Torah teacher for small children. Now one day Yankel decides he is sick and tired of being so poor in Eastern Europe and he wants to travel to America to change his fortune. And that is exactly what happens. He comes to the States, goes into business and becomes a wealthy man.

One night he is sitting comfortably in his posh mansion when he hears a pounding at the door.

"Who is it?" he calls out. He hears familiar voices calling out to him. "It's us, Yankel, yer ol' frens from Europe. Open te dur! Ve vant you to donate to our nu school!"

"Oh, no," Yankel yells out in horror. "They found me here!"

Yankel's *mazel* has changed but not the unique qualities he is meant to express in this world. In many ways Yankel has special sensitivities and characteristics that allow him to be at the forefront of advancing education in the world. He did not want to do that in the impoverished circumstances of Eastern Europe. Accordingly, he was able to change his fortune. However, his fresh challenge is whether he will use his new-found resources to further knowledge in the world by getting behind this educational program or will he just use his money for his own comforts and not realize his true potential.

Many books have been written over the past number of years advocating the idea that we create our own reality. There is truth to this idea and we need to realize that the things we do alter the circumstances of our lives. Our *mazel* is not set in stone; it is definitely affected and altered by our decisions and actions.

When Mazel Can't Change - Challenges That Are Part of Our Mission

I hope everything we said until now is completely clear because we are about to turn everything upside down. Just when you thought these concepts were lucid, we need to shake up the concept so that we can understand this on a higher plane. Here is a mystical story from the Talmud which seemingly contradicts everything we have learned.

There was once a very righteous Sage named Rabbi Eliezer ben Pedas who was extremely poor. One day he had to have a medical procedure done. After the procedure, he came home and searched the house for something to eat. To his chagrin, all he could find was a single piece of garlic. Since he needed to consume something and nothing else was available to him, he reluctantly ate the garlic. Soon he got weak and queasy and fainted. When his colleagues came to visit him, they saw him passed out on the floor. They observed that in his unconscious state he was making bizarre facial expressions, laughing, crying and "beaming."

They tried to help him wake up. When he finally opened his eyes, they tried to find out what had happened.

"We saw you crying, laughing and beaming when you were in an unconscious state. Do you know why?" they asked him.

Rabbi Eliezer explained that he had seen a vision where God was sitting with him. Rabbi Eliezer asked God, "How long will I continue to suffer in this world?" God empathized with this extremely righteous man who deserved so much good and asked, "Would you like me to turn the world back to the beginning and create it anew and maybe you will be born at a time of better *mazel* for sustenance and wealth?"

Rabbi Eliezer exclaimed, "What? You will completely redo the world and *maybe* my *mazel* will change? Please tell me," he continued, "have I lived most of my life or do I still have a majority of years to go?"

God told the Sage that he had already lived the majority of his years. At this point, Rabbi Eliezer began to cry and said, "If so, do not turn the world back." God now informed Rabbi Eliezer that in the merit of his choice, he would be given thirteen rivers of balsam oil as clear as the Euphrates and the Tigris for enjoyment in the World to Come.

Rabbi Eliezer began to laugh at the good news but then he contended with God further. "Thirteen rivers and no more?" God responded, "What will I have left to give your friends?"

Rabbi Eliezer responded, "Almighty, I am only asking to receive from the portion of those who do not earn their destiny." At that point in the vision, God playfully flicked Rabbi Eliezer on the forehead and those were the sparks the Sages saw beaming from his face.

This mystical story has many layers of hidden meaning: what do the thirteen rivers of balsam represent? Why did God flick sparks on Rabbi Eliezer's forehead? What does all this really mean? One particular aspect of this text is imperative for us to understand because it seems to completely contradict our whole presentation until now.

Rabbi Eliezer clearly wanted the Almighty to change his *mazel*. Now we can assume that Rabbi Eliezer earned the ability to have his *mazel* change based on his great deeds or perhaps even because of the prayers he offered throughout his difficult times. If so, why does God need to destroy the entire world and rebuild it from scratch to give him a better *mazel* for finances? Why can't God simply give him more money?

What makes the story even more bizarre is the fact that through God's recreating the world, Rabbi Eliezer's *mazel* may end up better, but it may not! Why is there a maybe? Isn't God Omnipotent and can't He make anything occur? What is the nature of this "maybe"?

The *Kabbalists* reveal to us a deep secret here. There are two different aspects to *mazel*. One is called the *Lower Mazel* (*Mazel Tachton*) and the other is called the *Upper Mazel* (*Mazel Elyon*). Until now, we have spoken about the *Lower Mazel*. The *Lower Mazel* is a means through which one can reach one's goal. If your unique destiny is to express your own brand of kindness, truth, dedication or holiness, the circumstances and tools you are given to get there (your *mazel*) can be changed under certain conditions. However, there is a deeper form of *mazel* that does not change; and that is your *Upper Mazel* (*Mazel Elyon*). The reason why that *mazel* can't change is because it is not just a "means" to an end. Rather, it is part of the ends itself!

Sometimes one's *mazel* isn't simply a tool to attain one's destiny but is an integral link to one's genuine destiny. For most people who have a *mazel* that doesn't allot them so much money, their actions can lead to a change of that *mazel*. In Rabbi Eliezer's case, his poverty was itself part of what he needed to reveal in the world. Rabbi Eliezer's challenge was to be destitute in this world and still be a happy, holy, and positive person. In his unique way, he was supposed to epitomize such an approach to the world. People could learn from him how to deal with the difficulties of financial challenges, the roots of being happy with what they have, the prioritization of the spiritual over the physical and many more lessons that Rabbi Eliezer's poverty created. This higher level of *mazel* touches the core of the human being, and *it is actually a reflection of the person's soul.*

Individual *Mazel's* Are Interconnected to Form a Grand Plan (the Mission of Humankind)

Visualize a jigsaw puzzle. Each piece interlocks with the others in a unique way to create the greater picture. Every distinct piece of the puzzle represents the special tasks that every individual in this world must accomplish. The task is determined by the root and essence of the person's soul. Just as a body is a unified whole and yet has diverse organs with distinct functions, so too our souls are interconnected and yet have differentiated roots and tasks. Consequently, the nature of the individual's soul will determine the specific task he or she is given. A person's mission or destiny will then require specific circumstances and details to express and bring his or her destiny to fruition.

These circumstances are what we have been calling *mazel*. When the details of these circumstances are not absolutely necessary to our destiny, this is what we call the *Lower Mazel* (*Mazel Tachton*) - one's *mazal* that can change. However, when the circumstances are integral to the expression of the destiny itself, what we call the *Upper Mazel* (*Mazel Elyon*), it cannot be changed. Rabbi Eliezer's unique task was so bound to his situation of poverty that if the Creator had changed his *mazel*, it would have actually affected Rabbi Eliezer's mission. If so, that piece of the human puzzle would have been lost and the entire puzzle would no longer be complete! This is comparable to buying a 1,000-piece jigsaw puzzle of a human face, putting it all together and then noticing that the nose is missing!

Every person has a unique mission and the entire system needs everyone to carry their own individual weight. Humankind was formed from one male/female being (as opposed to the animal kingdom, which was created with many individual creatures in each species) in order to teach us that each individual is an entire world. If you save one person, you save an entire world because each individual is literally a unique world with a unique mission that only that individual can accomplish.

That is exactly what God meant when He told Rabbi Eliezer, "I can rebuild the world and maybe you will come up with a better *mazel*."

Rabbi Eliezer's *Upper Mazel* was connected to his unique soul mission and if that changed, the whole system would have to change. The present picture would no longer be usable, and the world would have to be restarted with the root of Rabbi Eliezer still undetermined (5*).

Imagine a football team that can't win a game because they never protect their quarterback. As soon as the ball is snapped, the defense tramples over the front line and crushes the quarterback every time. The team loses one game after another. The coaches get together and watch the film from all the previous games and they notice something bizarre. The front lineman, Jones, instead of blocking against the onslaught of the defense, keeps running down the field leaving the quarterback open for disaster. They quickly call Jones into the office and ask him to explain his bizarre behavior. Jones elucidates his position, "I want to be one of those quick jolting running backs and that's why I run down the field, to be just like them."

The coaches grill him, "Jones, you are a 350-pound lineman. You have muscles on your eyelids! What are you talking about? You were made to play offensive line. You're a natural. And anyway, we don't need another running back. We need your skills on the offensive line."

It may be true that Jones envies the sleek running backs, but if he focuses on his unique gifts, he will realize what his mission should be. In fact, the tools that Jones was given are completely integral to his task. His size and strength are part and parcel of his mission, and the entire team needs his unique skill to win.

Let's review this train of thought:

1. The root of our soul is what determines our unique mission.

2. A person is given the tools (*mazel*) to accomplish his or her mission.

3. Sometimes the tools can change (*Lower Mazel*); alternative tools can accomplish the same mission.

4. Other times, the mission must be expressed through those specific tools; the tools are intrinsically connected with the mission, the *Upper Mazel*, and that *mazel* doesn't change.

Understanding Why Everyone's Mission Is Ideal (Including *Mazel*)

You may complain that this isn't fair. Why does he get to be the running back and not me? The simple answer is that the team needs all the various players and if you appreciate your uniqueness, you will love being you. Now, although you are probably willing to accede that loving yourself is a good idea, you may rightfully protest that this is starting to sound like a pseudo self-help guide. The realization that diverse components are necessary and that everyone has something special to offer doesn't explain why one person should have it so much harder than the other. It's not just that Rabbi Eliezer's role is different, it is seemingly inferior, and what makes it worse is that it really can't be changed!

To fully understand the concept in play here, we must get beyond our limited desires and realities. Since we all want the good life and do not fully realize that this world is actually a corridor to an eternal dimension, it can be hard for us to internalize the true reality. However, let's try to incorporate what we learned earlier and remember that our purpose in this world is to earn our ultimate station after this dimension.

Accordingly, the tools are just a means to an end. Although we are judged on the basis of what we do in this world, in a real sense **our effort is actually more important than the result.**

Imagine two people who each own a plot of land that has stones strewn about the property. Both people lift and haul the stones away in order to clear their land. But one owner has much heavier stones on his territory. In the end, the result may be the same. They both have clear fields. However, the man who lifted the heavier stones will certainly have developed bigger muscles than his neighbor.

Since we are here to perfect ourselves, when we expend greater energy, we will be developing ourselves even more. Therefore, if the tools we are given are difficult, we must realize that we will be paid back in kind. We will actually get a greater reward for having succeeded with such a difficult *mazel*. Rabbi Eliezer had a painful challenge, but God informed him, specifically in relation to his challenges, that there was tremendous reward after this world, this reality. If we truly understand this concept, it makes coping with the difficulties well worth it.

There is now a reverse problem, though, with this approach. We seem to be implying that Rabbi Eliezer and those who are righteous in spite of a challenging *mazel* get more eternal reward. But if that is true, then it sounds like it isn't fair to the righteous people who have it good! Most of us are grounded in this world and want our pleasures now, but a righteous person, a *tzaddik*, clearly recognizes the greater value of the world to come. Such a person will protest that it's not fair, but in the opposite way. "Why can't I have the great difficulties of Rabbi Eliezer? I would much rather have difficulties in this temporal reality than compromise my reward for eternity!"

The profound answer is *that every person's distinct challenges are the result of his or her unique being*, the root of his or her soul. Consequently, our difficulties and rewards are exactly suited to our needs! *And so our unique challenges become the special flavor, so to speak, of our eternity itself.* The entire series of life's challenges blend together to give us an exclusive composite of our being and that is our taste of eternity. The football lineman realizes in the end that the position he plays is part of the definition of who he is, and this becomes part and parcel of his pleasure in the game. So too, each person's unique situation is the expression of his or her being, and in the end that is **exactly what we can and want to experience!**

Let's try to elucidate this difficult concept. For those of us who are the couch potato types, let's remind ourselves of the incredible sense of embarrassment we feel when we watch the Paralympic Games. We will certainly see paraplegics doing things that we can only dream of. Yet, we must admit that even if the paraplegic changes his deeds or his name, normally speaking, he will not regain use of his legs. That is a reality that he must live with. Still, his success and sense of accomplishment is defined and enhanced *specifically because of his circumstances*. The stars of the Paralympic Games use the tools they have and demonstrate many lessons to the world. It becomes part and parcel of their greatness.

Similarly, our *Upper Mazel* is part of our uniqueness. It is true that in the World to Come the constraints of the individual's *mazel* will be lifted (and so too in our analogy, the paraplegic will no longer have disabilities), but the satisfaction and triumph one achieves by perfecting himself within those particular life challenges are experienced eternally. Our challenges will actually help form the flavor of our unique eternal pleasure that lasts forever; it will be special to us and serve as a true reflection of our inner essence.

To that end, we must realize and celebrate our uniqueness.

Imagine you received a call from the CIA. There is an urgent mission and the entire world's future depends upon the success of it. The CIA explains that if we succeed the world will live in peace and harmony, but if we fail the world will be destroyed. The CIA then proceeds to inform you that they have investigated the profiles of every human being on the planet and have concluded that you are the only person capable of doing the job.

How would you feel? You would certainly feel special and revel in your abilities. Yet this is exactly what happens to you each day! Since the Creator has a plan for the world and every individual has an exclusive task, it is as if the Creator is calling you on the phone and telling you that the whole world is depending on you to perform your mission. And in light of the fact that you are being chosen by an Omnipotent, Omniscient Being, you are obviously sufficiently qualified for the job! This is what the Talmud means when it says that everyone is required to say, "The world was created for me." This is not an egocentric position.

The statement is true for everyone. Each and every person is obligated to say that the world was created for him or her because it's *true*.

Everyone has a distinct destiny. Each of us is given the tools to bring out our unique task. We may use those tools and express our mission in any number of ways or we may receive different tools (*Mazel Tachton, Lower Mazel*) to bring out our special charge. In certain cases, our special task has to be expressed through the specific tools we have been given (*Mazel Elyon, Upper Mazel*), but either way, the system is designed to bring out our inner selves. When we overcome our challenges and maximize the tools we've been given, we have completed our mission and have reached our true destiny.

Application One:

In this chapter, we have discussed the idea of an individual's unique mission. There were some very interesting concepts, but our goal here is not just philosophy. We want to know how to better ourselves and our world.

So we should ask the obvious question: "How do I know what my unique mission is?" Great question! Unfortunately, it is an easier question to ask than it is to answer. In ancient times when there were prophets, this was one of the prophet's undertakings: to reveal to people the root of their soul and thereby their unique mission. Today, when there are no prophets, this search is a lifelong quest. Yet we have a clue how to solve this crucial mystery. Since the positive traits and the individual challenges we have are tools to achieve our destiny, if we clearly understand our individual traits, we will be closer to figuring out our mission.

Go into a quiet room. Bring the writing tools you like the most, whether it is a lap top, or a pencil, pen, magic marker and notebook.

List twenty-five descriptive words about yourself. For example: that you are kind, considerate, sensitive, loyal, devoted, a good friend, etc. You will see that the first few are easy, but soon you may run out of things to say. DON'T GIVE UP NOW! The problem may be because we are looking for things that are too grand.

Write down very simple, seemingly inane things. For example, things like: I am creative, I like music, I like nature, I am organized. These things on their own may seem insignificant, but after you have a list of twenty-five descriptive words, you will see the tapestry of yourself begin to emerge. Your list may show a combination of very different traits within your being. You are now getting a snapshot of the unique tools that you were given.

Read this list out loud every day for a week. Let your mind be open to new ideas of projects you may want to take on.

Additionally, in a relaxed meditative state, repeat a phrase that summarizes for you the concept that you have a special quality and mission that no one else can accomplish.

For example, you can say, "*Bishvili nivrah haolam*-בִּשְׁבִילִי נִבְרָא הָעוֹלָם- the world was created for me"; or, "God created me for a special purpose"; or any other expression that resonates this concept for you.

Repeat it until this concept becomes clear in your mind and instilled in your heart.

Endnotes

(1*) The Divine system favors the good. For instance, if a person has a negative plan and is prevented from carrying it out, it is not considered as if he actually did the act unless he has repeated that type of behavior numerous times before.

(2*) The Hebrew word for traits is middot. Amazingly, the literal translation of middot is actually "measurements" and not traits. The reason for this is that traits are neither good nor bad, rather it depends on what measure they are used in. There are times to be courageous and times to be cautious. If you are afraid of taking any chances, you are probably missing a lot of life; and if you are jumping off cliffs at every turn, you may easily end your life. The key is the balance of the traits and that they should be used in the right way and right measure. There is discussion among the Sages about whether any traits are intrinsically positive or negative. According to Maimonides, the traits of haughtiness and anger fit the negative criterion while the Chassidic masters believe that even they can be used to do what is good and right.

(3*) Avraham and Sarah's son is named Yitzchak (Isaac) which is spelled in Hebrew יִצְחָק The word itself means laughter, as laughter is generated when the opposite of an expected result happens. A good punch line always surprises you by going in an unforeseen way, so too Yitzchak's birth is laughter producing becomes it contradicts the expected. Additionally,

when we rearrange the letters of Yitzchak's name it spells קֵץ-חַי *(Ketz–Chai)* which means "end of life." This is because Yitzchak's existence (as well as that of his descendants) begins where life normally ends.

(4*) The essence of the person is actually his soul, in Hebrew "neshamah" נְשָׁמָה, whose central letters spell the word shem (שֵׁם) which means name. This is because a name in Hebrew encapsulates the essence of the entity. This is also evident in the root of the word neshamah (soul) which is shemamon שְׁמָמוֹן. Shemamon is something that cannot be described because it is incomprehensible to the one who observes it; it appears to the viewer as nothingness. This is because the essence of an entity, especially the soul, cannot be described. It is beyond words. A name is the handle by which we have some grasp on the core of an entity.

(5*) There is a possible phenomenon that one who completes one's distinct role can participate in fulfilling a role that another person refuses to do. This is what Rabbi Eliezer is asking God when he wants the reward of those who do not fulfill their destiny. Rabbi Eliezer is expressing his willingness to also take on their roles and responsibility, thereby entitling him to receive their potential reward. In our analogy, Rabbi Eliezer would become their jigsaw puzzle piece.

CHAPTER THREE

FREE-WILL AND PERSONAL GROWTH

....

In order to reach our destiny, as we have discussed, we must be able to make our choices freely and there must be a system that allows us to continuously grow to our full potential...

The shelves of every bookstore are lined with a plethora of self-help books. On the radio, TV, internet and in magazines everyone is talking about "growth." Yet what does it mean to grow? What is the key element in the growth process and what is the attitude necessary to continually grow in life?

Let's start by defining our terms. Babies and businesses both grow by getting bigger, but the growth we are talking about here has nothing to do with weight or size. So what is the connection between the two expressions? There is a *Kabbalistic* concept based on a verse in the Book of Job which says, "ומבשרי אחזה א-לוה-*Umisari echezeh Eloka* –from my flesh I will perceive Divinity." The incredible meaning of this verse is that through understanding the structure of the human being (the flesh), we can extrapolate to the structure of the entire Divine system. The fascinating upshot of this idea is that if we understand ourselves we will actually understand the whole universe. The reason that this is true is because the Omnipotent Creator built a multitude of spiritual worlds that are all reflection of one another, as well as a physical world which also parallels these spiritual dimensions. Each world is created on a different level and the flow is transmitted through these different dimensions until it reaches this physical world.

If you didn't understand what I'm talking about yet, don't worry, it will all be clear soon. But for now we need to realize that just as this physical world parallels the spiritual worlds, there is one entity in particular that is a microcosm of the entire system. This one entity has parts and components that parallel the whole universe; this entity is the human being. So if we want to understand the deepest most esoteric secrets we can start by contemplating the way we are built. The construct of a human being reflects the systems that the Omnipotent Source created; it is therefore a key to understanding.

So what happens when we physically grow? We expand ourselves as if we were pressing against the borders that confine us. Similarly, the spiritual process of growth has to do with pressing against the parameters that limit us, thereby enlarging our boundaries. Remember this concept because soon we will revisit this analogy between physical and spiritual growth in a more precise way than we may have previously imagined possible.

Crucial Factor Needed for Growth

Now let's explore and understand a related question about the nature of growth. What would you say is the most important thing needed for you to grow? There are obviously numerous candidates for this honor. Many traits are fundamental for a person's development: honesty, humility and determination, to name just a few. But there is one thing that is so central to our development that without it absolutely no growth can take place. I warn you though; the answer is going to sound very weird.

The most fundamental thing in the world to enable growth is concealment. Huh? Concealment is apparently the opposite of growth. Let me please explain. The word in Hebrew for world is *Olam*. Yet if we consider the etymology of the word we will realize that the word

Olam - world - is from the root *lehaOlem* which means to conceal or hide.

That is because the most central factor that makes this world look the way it does is "hiddenness." The *Kabbalists* explain how the Creator, so to speak, concealed Himself in order to create an apparently separate reality. The great mystery of how the finite is not completely subsumed and absorbed into the Infinite is at the center of *Kabbalistic* discussion and it revolves around the concept of "hiddenness."

Furthermore, concealment provides us with the ability to have free choice. For although a person is free to stick his hand into a fire or jump off a fifty story building, no normal person would do such a thing. *It is only when the alternatives are not so obvious that choosing correctly is meaningful.* (1*)

For example, there is an entity in creation that sees reality so clearly that it essentially has no free-will. This entity (in English) is called an angel. I actually hate using the word angels because it conjures up bizarre images of little guys with halos or pitch forks sitting on your shoulders. The reality is that the Creator built a system where the roots of the physical dimension are based in a spiritual realm. When any action or event takes place in the physical world it is first initiated in the spiritual worlds and, so to speak, transmitted until it reaches this physical plane. This step down system, where the "flow" moves from the highest spiritual dimension to the lowest in gradations was deemed by the Creator ideal to accomplish the purpose of the world. The forces in the spiritual dimension (angels, etc.) function with specific parameters similar to laws in the physical world. Angel in Hebrew is *malach*, from the root *malachah*, which means action, work or job, because these forces cause certain actions which conform to the laws of the spiritual world. They have no free-will.

One explanation for their lack of free-will is that they experience God so clearly that it is impossible to do anything counter to the Almighty's wishes. If it were perfectly obvious to us what was right or wrong, we would essentially be forced to do what is right because the alternative would be tantamount to putting our hand in the fire or jumping off a building.

Free-will requires concealment.

Concealment Gives Rise to the Possibility of Evil and Our Resistance to It Makes Us Great

Now this brings us to the central issue of trying to understand the baffling concept of evil. Many religions struggle with the idea of an all benevolent God that creates evil. In some religions there is a separate force that some call the devil that opposes God and proliferates evil. From a Jewish perspective such an idea is considered idolatrous. For there can be no other power in any way other than the Omnipotent Source.

Rather, the primary book on Jewish mysticism, known as the Zohar, explains the concept of Satan with a metaphor. Imagine a king that had a beloved son whom he trained to be a righteous man. The king wants his son to integrate all the valuable lessons that he has learned and put them into practice, thereby actually developing into a truly great man. So the king prepares the son, gives him a money pouch and sends him out into the great big world with directives on how to act morally. The king then goes and hires a prostitute to tempt his son. The prostitute is not functioning independently. She works for the king. She will do the assignment the king gave her because the king wants his son to act morally by his own choice.

And even as the prostitute is trying to tempt the son with all her persuasive powers, she herself wants the king's son to reject her; as this is the true desire of the king himself and will be the ultimate success of the son. Similarly, the Jewish teaching about evil is that it has no free reign. Rather, the Infinite One creates the reality of evil as part of His plan so that man can overcome it.

The potential for evil is so important in the plan of creation that the Torah text makes an eye opening variation when referring to the creation of this force. In the story of creation, the text says, "and God saw it was good" after each specific day of creation. However, on the final day of creation the text says "and God saw it was **very** good." The additional verbiage "very" comes to include the creation of the force of evil. Why would the creation of the force of evil be called "very good"? One answer is that without a force pulling towards evil there would be no possibility of free-will and consequently nothing to accomplish in the world.

Let's go even deeper and try to understand some aspect of how the Omnipotent One created the power of evil in this world. Obviously evil cannot be found or associated in any way with God. Therefore, the creation of evil originates **specifically through God concealing Himself**. This hiddenness allows for the formation of a system of evil. And when the Infinite Light is revealed the potential for evil will disappear.

Let me a share an analogy with you that may make this idea clearer.

Our family used to live in an apartment in Jerusalem. I always wanted my children to eat healthy foods so I tried to limit the amount of unhealthy treats they would have. In my zeal to make the point, I used to call candy, "junk" and my kids were only allowed "junk" at certain times. Unfortunately, since English wasn't my children's first language they didn't pick up that I was using a derogatory term for treats and actually grew up thinking candy was called "junk". So if some unwitting friend would ever give my kids candy he would be shocked by the kids' response, "Thanks for the junk, sir."

We even had a "junk closet" where the treats were kept. My kids knew that they couldn't take things out of the junk closet without permission. Then on one Shabbat my wife and I were sleeping late when I heard movement around the junk closet. It seems that my kids were helping themselves to the junk. Well I know my kids and they wouldn't just take something when they weren't allowed to. However, here they had a logical rationale to help themselves to the junk by telling themselves, "our parents are asleep and we don't want to wake them up, after all it's Shabbat morning and they can sleep a little later than usual. Besides, since it is Shabbat our parents would **want us** to have special treats." I have to admit that is a pretty good rationalization.

Hearing them party in the junk closet, I decided to quietly enter into that room. I stood behind the kids so that they couldn't see me and suddenly I loudly cleared my throat. They jumped! **They were busted in the junk closet,** caught with their hand in the proverbial cookie jar.

Let's try to understand this interaction. If the kids believed that they weren't doing anything unacceptable, why were they so darn guilty when I saw them? A minute beforehand, they were sure that they were doing the right thing and not only would I not be upset with them but I would commend them for their incisive judgment. Yet a moment later they are looking to flee the scene of the crime.

The difference is that when I was not in the room they were able to rationalize their actions, but once my presence was apparent they could no longer delude themselves. Imagine doing something negative when suddenly you perceptibly experience God's Presence. You would certainly desist from the negative act and be vigilant to do right. It is the hiddenness of the Omnipotent Source that allows an entity of evil to be created. If we were to see reality clearly our choices would change.

The Hebrew word to see *roah* - רָאָה - is the same root as יִרְאָה -*yireih* - which means awe or fear, because when we *see* things as they really are, we have the appropriate *awe* (2*). Our subsequent actions all comply with our new clarity of vision. This is the experience of the *malachim*, the angels, who have clear perception. Yet this is also one of the reasons the angels cannot progress, because these spiritual forces are static and incapable of developing, unlike human beings who can grow and change. They are said to have one leg, while humans have two. Although we imitate their spiritual prowess when we pray by keeping our legs together as if our legs were one, like the lofty angels, the uniqueness of humankind is that we can takes steps and grow. Their one leg represents that, unlike us, they cannot move forward. And it is specifically the option to resist evil that gives us the ability to move forward.

There are various terms for the forces of evil. Here are some you have heard of; the Angel of Death, Satan and the *Yetzer hara* (the Evil inclination). The Talmud tells us an amazing idea. **These forces are actually one and the same.** This is a very difficult statement to understand but if we apply what we have learned until now we can make some sense out of it.

So let's connect and summarize what we have learned.

1. It is specifically God's concealment that gives rise to the creation of evil.

2. The spiritual force (angel) that is created from that concealment is called Satan.

3. The concealment itself causes death because if we were able to fully comprehend our connection to the Eternal Source there would be no death in this world.

4. Death is thereby the result of the hiddenness that we are experiencing today.

5. Finally, on an individual level there is a personal manifestation of this force of evil tailored to each human being. This is called the *Yetzer hara* (the Evil inclination). When this hiddenness is revealed on the individual level it becomes every person's distinct and unique desire for negativity.

Hiddenness on a Personal Level (Our Own Negativity - *Yetzer Hara*)

Now we may be thinking, "I don't want to do evil; I'm a really nice guy." Well let me reframe this concept and substitute the word "counterproductive" for the word "evil." If we analyze ourselves honestly we will have to admit that there are different desires that rise up inside us all the time and some of these desires are for things that aren't good for us. So why would any normal, rationale being do things that are counterproductive and hurtful to them? Yet we do this all the time.

Pretend for a moment that you get home late one night. You should probably just crash, but instead you decide to raid the fridge first. You open up the freezer and lo and behold you find a pint of Ben and Jerry's ice cream.

You acquiesce to having just one spoonful, figuring, after all, what could be wrong with that? Then just one more scoop… then another… and another, until you realize that you have finished the entire pint! Now what? You get in your car and track down a 7/11 and buy a whole gallon, which you also manage to put away pretty nicely. The next morning your stomach is killing you and you barely fit into your clothes.

And yet we can do the same thing the next night… and the next… and the next. This is a clear manifestation of the *Yetzer hara*; the pursuing of desire in a way that is negative to our higher self. **Our *Yetzer hara* is the manifestation of God's hiddenness on our own personal plane.**

In addition to counterproductive desire, the *Yetzer hara* can also manifest as seeking power, honor and the like. This is a different expression of a person's *Yetzer hara* since there is no physical gratification of the senses. The root of these types of *Yetzer hara* actually comes from an impurity in the world that is a result of this concealment. Like a snake that gets no pleasure when it bites someone, we are sometimes pushed towards negativity without any real gain.

When we see a National Geographic nature show it is pretty amazing to see a baby horse or goat shortly after birth. They are soon running around and jumping all over. They somehow have a natural instinct of self-preservation that kicks in almost immediately. From early on they know how to protect themselves and flee from danger. On the other hand, when we take care of a child or infant, it is unnerving the amount of trouble the little fellow can get into. It almost seems like he is looking for the most dangerous and worst things to do. Our Sages reveal to us a most bizarre notion about this peculiarity in children. They say that the natural self-preservation mechanism is tainted by the *Yetzer hara*! There is an aspect of wanton harmfulness in a person that we can detect from the unwitting actions of a baby. This is the underpinning of the second type of *Yetzer hara* (3*).

A Text That Gives Us Insight into the Force of Negativity

Okay, so now that we have established that we have a *Yetzer hara*, let's delve deeper into this concept by studying the future of this force. The Talmud shares with us an amazing *Aggadic* teaching (see note 4* for definition) of what will be the end of the *Yetzer hara*. The Talmud reveals that in the future the Almighty will bring the *Yetzer hara* and slaughter it. The Prophet Zechariah referred to this event when he prophesized, "The entire land will mourn..." Wait a minute, that doesn't make any sense. If Zechariah is referring to the slaughtering of the *Yetzer hara* why should people mourn? They should rejoice!

We can understand this enigma through the teaching of the venerable Rabbi Yehudah. Rabbi Yehudah taught that in the future the Almighty will bring the *Yetzer hara* and slaughter it before the righteous and the wicked. To the righteous the *Yetzer hara* will appear like a giant mountain and to the wicked it will appear as a thin hair and both groups will cry. The righteous will cry and say, "How could we have overcome that giant mountain?" The wicked will cry and exclaim, "how could we **not** have overcome that thin hair?" The Almighty will wonder along with the righteous, as the verse says, "...If it will be wondrous in the eyes of the remnant of this people in those times, so too, it is wondrous in My eyes."

What is the meaning of this enigmatic riddle? What is going on in this story? The whole episode is completely bizarre. What does it mean that this force is being slaughtered? And then why was it created in the first place? Moreover, we still haven't answered the first question: why does the destruction of this force of negativity make people cry? I guess we can understand why the wicked are crying but we still have no idea why the righteous are sad. They should be throwing a party. The *Yetzer hara* has been compelling them towards negativity, and now it is gone! They were successful in conquering it, as the text says: they cry and say, "how did we overcome such a giant mountain?" Doesn't that indicate that they were successful?

But what is even more outlandish is the way the *Yetzer hara* appears differently to the righteous and the wicked. To the righteous it appears as a giant mountain and to the wicked it appears as a thin hair. That is backwards! The kind, wonderful people should have less negativity inside of them and their evil inclination should be like the thin hair. Shouldn't the evil people in the world who are always pursuing negative things and embroiled in base desires have an evil inclination as big as a mountain?

Lastly, the statement that the Almighty is wondering how the righteous were successful sounds almost sacrilegious. The Omnipotent Creator, by definition of Who He is, knows everything. It is one of the "requirements" of the job. So what could it possibly mean that the Almighty is surprised or amazed by the righteous people's achievements? And more confusing still, the text expresses God's wonderment as dependent on others: "if it is wondrous in their eyes... it is wondrous in My eyes." How can the Omnipotent One's amazement be contingent on our amazement?

As we have discussed, this world is based on concealment which allows us free choice. However, the goal is not to always remain in a state of hiddenness. Rather, hiddenness is a necessary ingredient in a process that allows us to be partners in the perfection of the world and ourselves. Just as a person who works a job has a time when he works and a time when he is paid, so too, in the greater scheme, there is a time of work, where the hiddenness is needed and a time of recompense, when hiddenness is contrary to the reward of clarity and perfection. Let's now look at the first stages of the time of reward, known as Messianic times.

The world is moving towards a time of clarity. We can see this in science as well as in the information and technological explosion. And although in many ways the world seems to be heading towards disaster, with new abilities to destroy the world and life many times over, we know that we are part of a process that can lead to greater clarity and a utopian society.

In the beginning of the utopian Messianic age the world will essentially function as it does today. However, there will be no war and famine because there will be tremendous clarity in the world. Knowledge will abound and people will plainly experience that there is One Source of existence. People will live long lives, in a world of peace and harmonious relationships. The entire Jewish nation will return to the Land of Israel and there will again be a central place, the Holy Temple in Jerusalem, where God's Presence will clearly be felt.

This ideal state of creation is not to be confused with the after-life. However, it is a period of time when we will experience the world in a rectified condition and it is a necessary stage in bringing about the ultimate time of reward (5*).

The key factor which characterizes Messianic time is the removal of concealment from this world. This is what the Talmud means when it says that the Almighty slaughters the *Yetzer hara* (6*), the evil inclination. When God will reveal Himself at that appointed time, evil can no longer exist. It is completely removed. This state is analogous to our earlier example of my children who pilfered the junk closet until I entered the room, at which point their rationalizations were no longer possible. When the Omnipotent One reveals Himself and the true nature of reality, the *Yetzer hara* is immediately eliminated.

Rabbi Karmi Ingber

An Equal and Opposite Resistance Is Required for Free-will and for Growth

Okay, that makes sense but it still doesn't answer why the righteous see the *Yetzer hara* as a giant mountain and the negative people see it as a thin hair.

So let's go further in our understanding of hiddenness. There is a verse in Ecclesiastes which states: *"Zeh le umas zeh asah Elokim* - God made everything parallel." The system of good parallels the system of negativity. This is necessary in order to have free-will. If the scales were tipped and we saw the truth clearly we would lose our free-will.

Let's now return to our original analogy between physical and spiritual growth. Imagine a man who wants to strengthen his muscles so he starts lifting weights regularly at the gym. He starts with ten pound weights. It is difficult for him but he is able to manage it.

In two weeks an amazing thing happens. Our weightlifter discovers that the ten pound weights are too easy for him. How can this be? Isn't he picking up the same amount as before? The answer is that as he becomes accustomed to the resistance, it no longer poses a challenge.

This is the secret to growth: to constantly work against the proper resistance.

Growth is attained when the amount of resistance we must overcome is difficult but still doable.

On one hand, if someone begins his work-out regiment by trying to lift 300 pounds on his first day he is certainly not accomplishing anything positive. And on the other hand, if someone's entire workout consists of lifting a cup of water everyday it is meaningless. Growth happens when you toil exactly at the proper point of resistance. *And when that level of resistance is mastered, you must increase the weight accordingly in order to continue growing.*

This is analogous to ground war tactics. The battle is located at the point where the two armies meet. As one side conquers new territory the battle line moves. The vertex of the battle is now conquered terrain.

Let's imagine that a child is born into a family of thieves. Let's call him Jerry. He is raised with the idea that theft is justified and he sees nothing wrong with a life of crime. All throughout his youth Jerry freely steals from classmates as well as stores. We can say that since Jerry doesn't even entertain the idea that stealing is wrong, it is considered to be beyond his "battle-ground point" (7*).

However, Jerry does realize that there may be something wrong with murder. He has never killed anyone and has some hesitation about it. One day, he is in the midst of a break in, and is about to be caught. He is now facing a very serious moment of truth. Will he kill the man who can identify him? Will he escape undetected? What will he do at *this moment?* He is in the midst of this theft and whichever way he decides to act, this will be a tremendous turning point in his life.

If Jerry decides not to murder, he has won that specific battle. But the challenge of murder is still not considered "conquered territory." Jerry is still stealing and is often faced with this potential predicament of killing to avoid being caught. After numerous times of facing this challenge of choosing not to murder someone, he is now resolved that he will definitely *never* stoop to be a murderer. If this decision is an absolute demarcation point, then we can say that "not being a murderer" is conquered territory for Jerry.

After Jerry surmounts this major challenge, as his life continues, he meets someone who speaks to him about the value of respecting personal property and not stealing. Jerry has never heard these ideas before, it is completely different than the viewpoint with which he was raised and how he has lived his whole life until this point. He never even considered that it was wrong to steal. This was his life! But as he reflects on the words of this person, he realizes that stealing *is* wrong.

He considers changing his life, even though he is surrounded by other thieves, his "colleagues" in this sordid profession. After overcoming numerous temptations to steal, Jerry's ethical mindset has developed to the point where he will never steal again.

Envision now that Jerry starts to advance spiritually. Step by step he develops until, eventually, he becomes a holy man. He now spends his day studying Torah and helping others. He learns the laws of proper speech and never speaks negatively about anyone ever again.

Jerry has become an exemplary human being. At each stage of his spiritual development the battle line keeps advancing. At the beginning of Jerry's journey, when he was still battling the urge to kill, if someone would have told him to avoid negative speech, it would have been nonsensical to him. It was still well beyond his battle ground, tantamount to a person trying to bench press a refrigerator on his first day of working out.

On the other hand, if a few of Jerry's old buddies from the gang would go to the new "Holy Jerry" and ask him to knock off a liquor store with them, he would be dumbfounded. He would ask them incredulously, "Why in the world would I want to do that?" That challenge is already conquered territory for Jerry; it's now like lifting a feather.

With every advance Jerry is getting stronger. The challenges of yesterday are obvious wins and simple to him today. So how does Jerry continue to grow?

Returning to our analogy of physical growth, the only way to continue to build muscle is by **increasing the weight you lift.** The only way Jerry can keep growing is if the challenges become greater. But how can his challenges become greater if he is no longer tempted by the same base desires of his past?

His *Yetzer hara* must now become subtler and more cunning to tempt him in new areas that are harder to overcome. So let's say Jerry is now a righteous scholar who no longer yearns for base things. The *Yetzer hara* may now try to entice Jerry to pursue honor. He may develop a craving for acknowledgement of his superior spiritual status. This craving of the *Yetzer hara* is very crafty because it no longer appears as a base desire. It is cloaked in what appears to be righteousness. In Jewish law we are commanded to honor a scholar because of the Torah knowledge he possesses. The honor accorded to the scholar is in actuality honor for the Torah itself. The *Yetzer hara* of the scholar can deceive him into believing he only wants the honor for the sake of the Torah when in reality he may want it for his own aggrandizement. That is a very difficult *Yetzer hara* to combat, yet it is precisely the greater new weight that our weightlifter is now required to lift. The analogy of physical growth and spiritual growth is complete.

We can now solve the riddle of how the righteous see the *Yetzer hara* as a giant mountain and simultaneously the evil people see it as a thin hair. As the righteous continuously overcome the challenges of the *Yetzer hara*, the *Yetzer hara* itself gets bigger so that the righteous can keep growing. At the end of time when truth is revealed, the righteous see the force that tried to derail them throughout life and they are amazed at its magnitude. It appears to them as a giant mountain from all the challenges that they went through and all the growth they achieved.

The negative people, on the other hand, didn't battle their *Yetzer hara*. In fact, in many cases it derails them from the start. This is the phenomenon of the "dirty old man." The dirty old man was once a *dirty young man* but that wasn't as disturbing or incongruous to people. In reality the dirty old man is exactly as he always was, he has not overcome the desires and baseness of his youth. His *Yetzer hara* knocked him off the path early on and he never recovered. So when such a person sees his *Yetzer hara* at the end of time, it is tiny like a thin hair. It has not developed at all; it didn't need to develop. One push and the negative people were off track forever. The negative people see this, cry and bemoan, "Why couldn't we overcome such a thin hair?"

This rationale still doesn't explain why the righteous are crying. They should be rejoicing that they succeeded against their temptations even though it had developed into a giant mountain. The righteous cry because now that their *Yetzer hara* has been revealed and destroyed, their ability to grow is also lost. As long as there is a counter resistance to conquer, there are new vistas to reach. Now that there are no challenges the game is over. This explains a strange verse in the prophets which states, *"Yamim she'ain bahem chafetz* - days when they have no longing," which our Sages say refers to Messianic times.

How can a verse that talks about "days without longing" refer to a time that we specifically yearn, hope and pray for? The answer is that the two different dimensions have different objectives. Now is the time of work and then there is a time of reward. Although the Messianic age is not the ultimate reward it does usher in the time of eternal reward (*Olam HaBa*) and so the stage of work has significantly changed. The righteous cry because their period of earning is no longer the same. They are now acutely aware of that significant loss. (8*)

Free-will Growth Does Not Preclude Divine Assistance

One question still remains unresolved. Why does the Omnipotent One "wonder" with the righteous how they could have overcome the giant mountain? I understand that the people are shocked because they didn't realize how their *Yetzer hara* had grown and they can't believe that they succeeded. But the Omniscient Source should not be "wondering." Moreover, God links His wondering with the righteous people's wondering, as the verse says, "if it is wondrous in your eyes it is wondrous in My eyes too."

We have established that we need to freely choose our own path in order to accomplish the purpose of creation; yet that doesn't mean that the Source is not involved in the process.

Imagine you are the owner of a large business. Although you want your employees to earn their wages, sometimes, for numerous reasons, you help them beyond what they deserve. Let's say an employee has done great work in the past but is going through a difficult time in life. It is appropriate to help the employee get through this glitch not only because you may like the employee but because their past performance entitles them to some assistance now. Alternatively, if you have an employee that has not worked well but you believe that helping this employee now will inspire him to do better in the future, you may choose to help him based on your future hopes.

The Omnipotent Source wants to give us the ultimate pleasure and earn our connection to Him. In fact, this "will to give" is the motivation for creation. Yet as opposed to other belief systems, Judaism maintains that although God constantly gives us, He does it in a way that simultaneously maximizes our self-earnings. He does not just grace us because we are unworthy and sinful. That is not a Jewish belief. The view that man cannot succeed in overcoming negativity and therefore can only be saved by grace is a Christian idea. According to Christian theology, God's Torah was abolished because the sinful nature of mankind made it impossible to uphold. The Christian view asserts that they were freed "from the curse of the Law."

The Torah perspective, however, states that the Omnipotent One's infinite kindness assures that we can attain greatness through the impact of our deeds, thereby completing the purpose for creation.

There are spiritual principles and systems that the Divine Wisdom created that allow us to earn the good with the best chances of success.

Here are three examples:

1) Negative consequences are not meted out immediately.

2) Negative consequences are not meted out fully at one time.

3) There is a system of *teshuvah* (repentance or returning) in which we can rectify things we have done wrong.

These principles allow us to make mistakes and still earn our way. Although someone who would disobey a human king would be obliterated immediately, we make mistakes and yet continue to exist. This gives us time to correct our mistakes. If we do not fully rectify what we have done wrong, the negative consequences can be received in small steps to allow us the ability to continue. This is analogous to a person receiving a million-dollar loan from a benevolent donor. If the donor sees that the borrower is using the loan unwisely he sets up beneficial conditions that the borrower will be able to meet. The lender does not ignore the loan for a long time and then suddenly demand all the money in one day. Rather the kind lender will set up tiny payments to be paid back over a very long period of time. This procedure allows the borrower to maintain his dignity and pay back the loan. But it is only possible because of the incredible kindness of the lender. This process will be explained further in a later chapter.

Returning to our mystical text, when the righteous see the *Yetzer hara* as large as a mountain, they can't believe that they successfully vanquished it. In reality, however, it wasn't just their great prowess that did it; the Omnipotent One was guiding them every step of the way, assisting them in their travails and pointing them in the right direction. So when they marvel at their great success, God could easily burst their bubble by pointing out how His Divine Providence continuously rescued and guided them. But He doesn't do that. Instead He says, "If it is unbelievable in your eyes it is unbelievable in My eyes too." This means that although the Omnipotent One can take the credit for our successes, since we have acted according to the systems He created, we are credited as if we did it all ourselves!

Let's apply these methods of blending our earning with God's compassion into a practical scenario. But first let me add one more rule to the system. There is a rule that "if we open our hearts like the eye of a needle, God will open our hearts like a giant hall."

Now let's imagine that these righteous people at the outset of their journey opened their hearts slightly, and God now assists them by opening their hearts even more. They then make good choices and do good deeds. These positive steps protect them in times of weakness (like our good employee example). Let's say these righteous people then make mistakes. They receive some negative response that doesn't completely overwhelm them but does give them perspective to reassess their actions, i.e., and do *teshuvah*, repentance.

And so they continue to grow; all the time being supported and nurtured by Divine Providence. This is the deeper meaning of the idea that the Almighty wonders with them. The righteous marvel at what they have accomplished and God says, "Although I have helped you through out; I will marvel with you and give you all the credit because you have fully done your part." (9*)

I remember my first visit back to the States after learning Torah for a year and a half in Israel. I was taking a long train ride to Trenton, New Jersey. I saw an elderly religious Jew on the train and I sat down next to him. The man engaged me in conversation and told me that he was a Holocaust survivor. He asked me for my background and if I was always an observant Jew. I explained to him my diverse background and that my path had recently led to greater Jewish observance. He was genuinely impressed. He said that he didn't know if he had the gumption to overcome all the challenges of secular society as I did. He asked me how could it be that I was exposed to a society that had such different values than observant Judaism and that I could still see my way clearly enough to choose the spiritual path. I explained to him that I was always a seeker and I was always searching for truth. At this point in the conversation not only was he impressed with me but I was also feeling pretty smug about myself.

As we continued talking, he asked me where my parents were born. I explained that they were Holocaust survivors too. They were young children when the Holocaust began. Their parents and many of their siblings were killed in the death camps. At that moment the man's countenance changed and he became very stern and solemn. He shook his head and deplored me, "Don't tell me stories that you connected back to your heritage because you were a seeker. That is a lie!"

I was shocked by the accusation. He continued his barrage and declared, "The reason why you have increased your connection to Judaism is because your grandparents are in the heavens screaming, 'What has happened to my children?' Your connection to Judaism is in their merit, not your own." I looked at him with a glazed stare. I had been deflated just like a popped balloon.

This encounter made me realize the truth of his words. The more I thought about my life and all my decisions up until that point, I realized deep down that he was right. I may have made some good choices along the way but I had certainly received a lot of Divine assistance.

Let's put it all together now.

1. To accomplish our purpose in life we are given the free-will to choose.

2. Every time we choose correctly we gain strength and stature.

3. To ensure that we continue growing, the Omnipotent One consistently gives us new challenges so that we can become even greater and be the "owners" of our destiny.

There is one more crucial piece of information that we must work into this equation: that God gives us exactly the appropriate test we need. Our potential growth is personally tailor designed by the Omnipotent One so we can continuously climb to the highest heights. We are on a path; hopefully growing step by step. Each stride is specifically calculated for each of us at our **present** stage. So even though sometimes it seems too difficult or painful for us, we can remember that this test is designed expressly for our own good. We are not given a challenge we cannot triumph, though the definition of success is not always what we imagine. Understanding this truly transforms how we relate to our difficulties and can inspire us to become the people we were always meant to be.

Application One:

Anyone who has ever worked out at a gym has heard the phrase "no pain, no gain." Our society understands this lesson in the physical realm but unfortunately not in the spiritual. Often when you have to make a proper moral decision it runs contrary to your personal desires and it is therefore painful (especially at the outset of the spiritual path). That doesn't mean it's not correct. If anything, it may be a sign that it *is* correct.

Think of a moral dilemma you are facing, or better yet, proactively choose an act that you think would be spiritually honorable that you don't feel like doing.

Close your eyes and weigh out intellectually what you "should" do.

Assuming you have decided to do the moral or spiritual act, now deal with the part of you that doesn't want to do it (the *Yetzer hara*).

Feel the heaviness or discomfort of your body at doing the act and realize that overcoming this specific block is an expression of your power and greatness.

Sense yourself lifting this weight or overpowering this discomfort just like you would do so when lifting weights or doing aerobics in the gym. Meditate on that.

Tell yourself, "I have the ability to conquer my blocks and this is my opportunity. If it feels hard for me, this has all the more value!" Repeat this message with the words getting louder and clearer until you are at home with the message.

See yourself successfully accomplishing that act. See yourself the way you want to be. Imagine becoming the person you can be through your successful choices. Enlarge the picture in your mind, add color if you want, make it a motion picture if that enlightens you. After the vision is powerful and comfortable in your mind, step into the picture and sense how it feels to be that person.

Take your time and go through this process until it is comfortable and complete.

The Talmud teaches us that certain things in the world cannot be dealt with too harshly. The *Yetzer hara* is one of those things. If you try to "kill" your *Yetzer hara*, it will snap back at you. So if you still feel any block to doing the positive spiritual act, throw your *Yetzer hara* a figurative "bone." Figure out how you can give something to the part of you that doesn't want to do what you know is right. For example, if you are eating poorly and you are trying to make a change in that area, think of what you should be eating. Do the mental and emotional work we outlined above and **then give yourself some special treat to appease your *Yetzer hara*;** maybe say you are going to go to a special delicious (healthy) restaurant at the end of the week to celebrate your diet. Do this approach with whatever is the particular block of your *Yetzer hara*.

Application Two:

As we have seen, to grow you need to always expand your boundaries and push past your resistance. We also saw that challenges are tailor made for you to keep growing and becoming the person you can be.

Imagine that last night the Almighty appeared to you in a dream and told you exactly the challenges you were going to face the next day. Imagine every detail of the day's problems that were delineated: the morning coffee would spill on you, you would have to change your clothes and be late for work, your boss will yell at you, everything you try to accomplish at work will fail. However, God also tells you that the purpose of these difficulties is to see how you will react. God tells you that every time you take it in stride and don't get angry or frustrated you will be rewarded.

Now if you woke up in the morning and it happened just like that - your coffee spilled on you - what would be your response? Would you get mad? No way. You would be completely calm, cool and "happy." You would experience the problem as an opportunity to grow.

Okay, so let's try it. See yourself in your mind's eye responding in a positive way now that you know it's just a test. Step into that picture of yourself and experience how it feels to be a person who can deal with difficulties so smoothly. Now tell yourself that everything that happens to you is an opportunity to grow and it is tailor made for you. Meditate on this idea until you are comfortable with it.

Now try the experiment. Only allot an amount of time you think you can handle. Start with a few hours, or a half day when you approach every actual challenge of the experiment period with this understanding and positive attitude. Smile when something goes awry and understand it is an opportunity to grow. See everything that happens to you during that time frame as a chance to develop by processing things in this new way.

At this point it is best to do the exercise with only relatively simple problems. Eventually you can bring this approach fully into your life.

Endnotes

(1*) In Judaism, the after-life is called the world to come. But if the world to come is a time of clarity and endless connection to the Infinite, why is the word "Olam"- world, used, when this word really means hiddenness? This dimension is precisely supposed to be the removal of hiddenness. The reason is that the concealment that will remain will allow us to still retain our own existence even though we will be completely connected to the Infinite. A candle that approaches a giant flame becomes subsumed in that flame, the paradoxical wonder will be that even with the complete absorption into the Infinite flame we will still somehow retain an identity as an individual candle (we will discuss this in a later chapter).

(2*) This concept is codified in Jewish Law. A person who wants to be righteous is urged to "see" in his mind's eye at all times the Tetra-grammaton, the spelling out of God's Divine Name. The ability to actually see this Name before us consistently gives us the proper awe to live our lives on a completely different plane.

(3) Sigmund Freud seemed to have recognized these two drives in the human being. Freud defined the central psychological component, the "Id", in a similar way to the Yetzer hara of desire, while the Yetzer hara of destruction and impurity he deemed the "Death Wish." However, Freud's classifications in essence are very contrary to the Torah in that he defined the "Id" as the essential person and the "Super Ego" as psychological control imposed by culture and family. The Torah view is very different. The Yetzer hara is more akin to a mere reflection of the true self, intended to stimulate the actualization of the **higher self**. The higher self is really the soul and is more closely aligned with the Yetzer Tov, the spiritual agent that pushes us towards good. In Freud's system the Yetzer Tov is simply your externally imposed constraints, the Super Ego, while the Torah defines the Yetzer Tov as the positive motivator for the higher self and akin to your essential self.*

(4*) An Aggadah is mistranslated as a legend. It is misunderstood that way because the Aggadah is a fantastical account using a story, tale or metaphor. Yet we must understand why the Aggadah has such a fantastical nature. The Talmud itself is the embodiment of the oral Torah. The written Torah (the five books of Moses, plus the Prophets and the Writings) is cryptic, sometimes seemingly contradictory and seemingly full of omissions. The Torah cannot be understood without its companion component, the Oral Torah, which is primarily the book of the Talmud.

Those that are astute amongst us may have just noticed a glaring contradiction. How in the world could the book called the Talmud be part of the oral Torah; if it's a book, it's not oral! The answer is that the explanation of the Torah that was handed down to Moses on Mount Sinai was supposed to be transmitted orally. Oral transmission has many advantages over passing on a book. An oral transmission requires learning from a "living Torah," a human being that encapsulates the lessons of the Torah and shows you how to make them real. It necessitates memorizing and assimilating the information fully, to name a just a few benefits.

If you would retort that Oral transmission has the tremendous danger of becoming a game of broken telephone, there are two responses to that concern. First, in the kids' telephone game you whisper inane statements like, "Sally has a red bow." And that message inevitably gets lost. Imagine I whispered to you a message that told you where to find ten million dollars and how to prevent the world from being destroyed. Additionally, everyone in the chain is told and fully understands that their future and the future of the entire world now rests on their successful transmission of the message. With that kind of "telephone game," you would make sure to get it right.

Second, the Oral Torah is consistent, so the information needs to fit on all levels. Furthermore, it isn't just transferred from one source to another with one whisper. It is learned in its entirety by a nation and then reviewed consistently before their teachers until the teacher perceives that the student is a worthy and complete transmitter of the message. At that point he ordains his student. All that being said, the transmitters of the Oral Torah reached a point in Jewish history when the exile was about to grip the nation in a way it had never done before. The Sages became concerned that the tremendous suffering in exile could negatively impact the vital transmission of even a single law. This kind of loss or confusion would be, in essence, a type of destruction of the world.

So through Divine Providence, amidst the Roman Persecution, there was a respite in the form of a righteous Roman emperor who was a friend to the Jews. He is called Antoninus, in Jewish writing, and historians believe he is synonymous with the benevolent Emperor Marcus Aerilios. Marcus Aerilios was a very different Emperor than many of the other Roman leaders. He did not marry his horse or any other farm animal, nor did he play the fiddle while his city was burning. All of this in itself would have been a tremendous step up. But moreover, Jewish writings tell us that Marcus Aerilios was a close friend and student of the leading Sage of the time, Rabbi Yehudah the Prince. This political protection allowed Rabbi Yehudah to convene all of the Sages of Israel together and commit to paper the Oral Torah. It was not ideal that this had to be done but the Sages saw that it was necessary for our survival.

There were two parts of the Oral Torah that needed to be encapsulated; one focused on the law and commandments while the other focused on the esoteric and moral teachings.

However, there was a problem committing the deeper esoteric life lessons to writing. When this wisdom remained oral a teacher could refuse to teach it to any unworthy student. Now that the Oral Torah was to be written down it would be accessible to all. The Sages were very concerned that these profound teachings could be used by an unscrupulous person in a negative way. They therefore chose to shroud the concepts in riddles and fantastical parables to conceal the deeper teachings from the uninitiated. This is the Talmudic section called the Aggadah. Many misunderstand this to be ordinary legends.

If we look at the word Aggadah itself – אגדה, we notice an interesting progression. The letters are sequential from the beginning of the Alpha Bet, in English the equivalent of ABCDE. The only problem is the second letter, bet, is missing. אבגדה. The simple sequential flow represents the seemingly simple story line or legend but in actuality the parable is hiding the deepest of secrets. This is represented by the missing second letter Bet – ב. Every letter in the Hebrew Alpha Bet has a numerical value and the value of the second letter is 2. This represents that the deeper meaning of the Aggadah is hidden unless it is uncovered by the dialectic learning process of a Sage and the disciple. The inner meaning can only be transmitted through those that have been given the understanding of the riddle. The missing number 2 represents the key to understanding the secret, the transmission from teacher to student.

(5*) The Talmud records two different opinions on how the age of the Messiah will look. One opinion is that the essential difference is that the Jew will no longer be in exile and truth in this world will no longer be

concealed. However, the world will still continue according to its normal processes. This is the opinion we have quoted above. Still, there is a second opinion which speaks about Messianic times in a much more fantastic and supernatural way. As is the rule with all Talmudic arguments, both opinions are correct but just express different necessary and complimentary perspectives. The supernatural system of the Messianic times is a dynamic that comes about if we bring about this age through our own actions.

Our tradition teaches us that there are different ways the Messiah can come; either through the righteousness of our deeds or through God's appointed time (whether we merit it or not) and even a combination of the two where God compels us to improve our ways. This includes the concept that we will wake up because of the fear of an evil tyrant who will threaten our existence. If we do not bring about this era through our good actions, it will take on the more natural expression. Additionally, the period of Messiah can start out in the more natural mode and progress to the supernatural way as the world becomes more perfected. However, this is still not what we refer to as the world to come. That we will explain further in a later chapter.

(6*) The term "to slaughter" has two different connotations; one idea is simply the destroying of an entity while the second idea implies the very specific way we kill an animal to make it kosher. If an animal dies in any other way, it is forbidden. This parallels the two different types of Yetzer Hara, the Evil Inclinations that exist in the world. One Yetzer hara is the drive for power, honor, and haughtiness while the second Yetzer is desire. The Yetzer hara for power and control is killed and removed from the world, but the Yetzer hara for desire is not destroyed but rather refined and transformed into the yearning to attain truth and good. This is the reference to ritual type slaughter; through that process desire will remain in the world in a usable and solely positive form.

(7*) We are not dealing here with the notion that a human being has a moral compass that can help intuit right and wrong. There is certainly such a power which is an expression of an individual's neshamah (soul) and Yetzer Tov (inclination towards good). From the Divine perspective

everyone will be judged according to their unique situation and the challenges they had in tuning into that part of themselves; but here we are rather dealing with the reality that exists for a person that is unconscious of what is morally reprehensible (whether through his actions or upbringing). It is "practically" at this moment not really a possibility in his mind.

(8*) *During King Solomon's reign, "when each man dwelt beneath his vine and his fig tree," there was a taste of the future Messianic time. Indeed, the Sages teach us that during this period there were no famines or disasters in the entire world. The world enjoyed peace, tranquility and harmony. And similar to what will be during the Messianic era, people lived to ripe old ages. There was a Temple in Jerusalem where God's Presence was apparent to all. However, another comparable feature to Messianic times was that free-will was impaired due to the abundant clarity. Consequently, conversions were generally not accepted as many people wanted to join the Jewish people because of the lucidity of the era.*

(9*) *Rav Tzadok HaCohen notes that when the text refers to the people who are amazed by their success it calls them Tzaddikim (righteous people), as opposed to Baalei Teshuvah (people who have become righteous specifically through repenting from their negative ways). This is because those who have lived righteously throughout their lives can mistakenly take more credit than they should for their decision making. The Baal Teshuvah, who is quite aware of his shortcomings, clearly sees God's direction in his life and so is never amazed or enamored by his own success. He attributes everything to Divine guidance due to his unity (Devakus) and self-negation (Hitbatlus) to God. The Baal Teshuvah successfully perceives himself as a conduit to accomplish the Infinite will.*

CHAPTER FOUR

INDIVIDUAL FREEDOM
AND THE DIVINE PLAN

We now understand that the world has a purpose and we can achieve that purpose by choosing correctly to bring out our unique mission. But what happens when our free-will choices contradict the Divine plan or a Divine decree? To understand this, we need to unlock the mystery of individual freedom and the Divine plan…

Have you ever had the experience where someone does something against you that you consider terrible, but in the end it worked out for the best? How are you supposed to relate to and understand such a situation? Do you go over to your boss, girlfriend, boyfriend, neighbor, co-worker or relative and say, "Thank you for treating me so badly, my life is much better now because of it"?!

We see this dynamic happened in one of the great sagas of the Torah between Joseph (in Hebrew, Yosef) and his brothers. Yosef, the kid brother, is favored by their father Jacob (in Hebrew, Yacov), which causes the brothers to be envious of him. Yosef exacerbates the problem by telling his father all the negative things he believes his brothers are doing. An obviously explosive situation is brewing even if Yosef's intentions are completely altruistic. His brothers certainly don't believe they are. The brothers interpret Yosef's actions as an attempt to destroy them and they decide that he must be removed. Their jealousy clouds their judgment and they believe that as an act of self-defense Yosef should be killed. Then they mitigate his sentence and agree to sell him as a slave to merchants going to Egypt. Afterwards, remorse sets in. Many years later, famine hits the land of Israel (then called Canaan). The brothers must descend to Egypt to procure food, and are resolved to find and redeem Yosef from Egypt.

To their shock Yosef has risen from slave to ruler and he is now the viceroy of Egypt. After their amazing reunion, the brothers are scared that Yosef will take revenge upon them. They fall before him and request that he forgive them and not retaliate. Yosef responds, "Do not fear. Am I in God's place? Although your intentions were for bad, God thought it for the good in order to send me here to save many lives." Yosef assures his brothers of his positive intentions towards them. He supports and protects them for the rest of their lives.

Contained in this interaction are the keys to understanding the great conundrum of free-will and predeterminism. As we have discussed earlier, certain things may be predetermined and yet we have free-will. So if in the grand cosmic plan Yosef needs to go to Egypt where he will save the land from famine, does that absolve the brothers from the responsibility of selling him to Egypt? Can the brothers defend their action by claiming to God that God Himself obviously wanted and decreed that Yosef be sold to Egypt? Similarly, God told Avraham that his children will be slaves in a foreign land, so does that exonerate the Egyptian nation for the crime of enslaving the Jews? Imagine an Egyptian slave master arguing in the Heavenly court, "Hey I was only fulfilling what You wanted, I should be rewarded not punished!"

We Choose and Thereby Become Conduits

Let's understand the first level of how there can be a Divine decree and yet people have free-will. Imagine there is a decree that the Jewish nation will be slaves and tortured in a foreign land. Now let's even assume that the foreign aggressor is going to be Egypt. Does that mean that each and every Egyptian needs to be the one who will afflict the

Jews? No, definitely not. This principle is called *MaReshaim Yatzu Resha*, which means that evil people are chosen to become the conduit for evil decrees. This principle is borne out from an extremely strange verse in the Torah. The verse warns a person who builds a house to put a parapet on his roof (this is referring to a flat roof that people utilize like a modern penthouse apartment). The text even provides a reason, "lest the faller will fall off the roof." What kind of bizarre phrase is used here? It should say "lest a **person** will fall off the roof." Why are we calling him a "faller" even before he has fallen? The Talmud posits an amazing insight: this person was destined to fall for some other reason; that is why he is called "the faller." But our responsibility is to avoid being the agent for this tragedy. If you are careful about human life and build a fence on your roof, then you will prevent the "faller" from falling off *your* roof. If you are a negligent person who does not care about human life enough to secure your roof, you may become the instrument for the "fallers" demise.

Let's understand the upshot of this approach through a dialogue between the great Sage Rabbi Yossi and a Roman noblewoman. The Roman noblewomen scornfully asked Rabbi Yossi, "After God created the world what does He do all day?" Rabbi Yossi responded, "He brings couples together." The women laughed and said, "That isn't a big deal! I myself can do that easily."

So the noblewomen took a thousand of her male servants and matched them with a thousand of her female servants and arranged a mass wedding. The next day she saw her servants were a mess; emotionally and physically, beaten and bruised. The servants pleaded, "Please separate me from this person, I can't bear another moment with them." Upon seeing this, the Roman noblewomen said to Rabbi Yossi, "I now understand your answer that God is busy making matches! It is very true."

Now this whole discussion is strange. What did the Roman noblewomen want in the first place and what does Rabbi Yossi answer her? Is that what God really does all day? And finally, how did the failed marriages convince the noblewomen? Sometimes marriages don't work out, especially with little preparation beforehand!

First, we must understand that the Omnipotent One is not bound by time or our temporal concepts in any way, so the question "what does God do all day after creation" is absurd. But on a deeper level the Romans were pointing out a fundamental difference between Jewish thought and other religions. Other cultures believe that God is oblivious to what happens in this lowly world. He is too lofty to care about our individual problems.

This is completely false.

Philosophically it's actually backwards. Since the Omnipotent One is all powerful it isn't any "harder" for Him to know, direct and interact with every detail of the universe than not. And since the purpose of creation itself is dependent on how we relate with the world, God is totally involved in every aspect of life.

This is the deeper meaning of Rabbi Yossi's answer that God "brings couples together." Rabbi Yossi was not only referring to bringing people together but he meant that the Creator is bringing all the seemingly disparate things in this world together. The degree of exactitude of these cosmic matches is well beyond belief; from a person who deserves to lose money to a person who deserves to find it, from ancestors that are due recompense to descendants that receive it generations later, every possible combination in the world is being directed aptly by the Omnipotent Source. **Our free-will decisions are crucial factors in the Divine plan. Still, the Director of the universe guides and arranges it so that everything ends up exactly as it should be.**

One of the greatest manifestations of the intricate nature of how "seemingly" disparate things are united is the joining of a couple. Often when a couple become united and see how perfectly suited they are for each other, they are amazed by the series of events that brought them together. In fact, sometimes God has to turn the world upside down to unite these individuals (1*). The Roman noblewomen understood this lesson clearly once she saw the abysmal failure of her arbitrary match making attempt.

According to this, we can understand how things are "meant to be" and yet people have free-will.

Let's say Sam has been decreed to fall off a roof for some reason or other. If Paul is a negligent person who disregards the value of human life to the point where on his free-will scale he is capable of negligent homicide (although he would never murder someone intentionally), Sam's decree may be brought out through Paul. Paul, on a certain level, is a willing partner to this type of act. He does not build a fence on his roof and consequently **the match is made:** Sam falls off Paul's roof. And so too, any particular Egyptian that was cruel and enslaved a Jew cannot exonerate himself by saying it was meant to be. Our response to the Egyptian will be: it is true the Jews were decreed to be enslaved **but you didn't need to be the one to do it.**

Okay, that seems acceptable; but there is still a problem here. Let us assume for a moment that every Egyptian has the ability to choose if they will be a cruel enslaver of the Jews or not. What would happen **if all the Egyptians** would freely choose not to enslave the Jews? Then the decree would not come to fruition in Egypt at all.

Now if that is true, then we are back to where we started from. The Egyptian that "subjugates" the Jew can ask for reward instead of punishment because he's one of the few that is fulfilling the decree!

Free-will and Omniscience

To understand this conundrum, we need to digress a moment to a related but somewhat different problem. This is the age old paradox of God's Omniscience and our free-will. Since God knows exactly what I will do and His Knowledge is perfect, it is impossible for me to do anything else. If the Omniscient One knows that I will continue writing this sentence **now** I must do it because what He knows will happen must come to pass. If what He knows will happen does not come to pass, that would mean that His knowledge is flawed and that is impossible, since God by definition must be Omniscient and perfect in every way.

"Oh no," you realize, "If that is true - *I must do what He knows I will do* - then there really isn't any free-choice and consequently no purpose in the whole creation!" Not a good conclusion at all.

Don't get too nervous though. We do have free-will and so there is purpose to the universe. Let's try to unravel this dilemma. We'll first revisit an amusing paradox you probably heard when you were a kid: "Can God make a rock so heavy that even He can't pick it up?"

If you were a philosophical kid, you may have wasted many hours trying to figure this one out. But in reality it is a foolish question.

Your inner child may be annoyed and getting angry at me now, thinking, how dare I call your childhood questions foolish?

Let me explain.

If you were in outer space would this paradox be so perplexing? Not at all. Since there is no gravity in outer space, the question itself is nonsensical. The paradox only makes sense in our world where there is gravity and thereby weight. In our world you can talk about an object that is so heavy that it can't be lifted but in a weightless universe the question itself is absurd. Similarly, when you ask how the Omniscient One can know what I'm going to do and yet I can still choose freely, you are comparing your knowledge to the knowledge of the Limitless One. However, in reality we have no concept of His knowledge. Human beings and their knowledge are not *one*; we are people who *have* knowledge. So when we learn something new, we add something to our knowledge base. But this is not true of God. As the Sage philosopher Maimonides puts it, "The Endless One is the knower, the knowing and the knowledge." He and His knowledge are one and just like we can't understand Him at all we can't understand how He knows. Just as our limited sense of sight cannot see 'sound' so too our limited understanding has no way to grasp how the Infinite One knows. **So however He knows; that does not force or determine our choices.**

Confused? Let me give you a variation on this idea that may be a bit more comprehensible. When we speak about the afterlife and its being infinite, our limited minds imagine that it will be a long, long time; so much time that it will continue on forever. This perception is incorrect and it's based on the fact that we are 'stuck in time'. All of our conceptions are time bound because that is the only thing we know. If we think about it, we realize that we only really experience the fleeting moment of the present. The past exists in our memory and the future is in our imagination.

And so the concept of infinity doesn't mean that we will keep experiencing the fleeting present on and on; **rather we will experience the past and the future as we experience the present right now.** That is a truly eternal moment! And if we find this idea mind boggling, it is precisely because our present day reality is constructed completely within time and space. Obviously God is not limited by the time and space He created.

In fact, the Tetragrammaton (God's essential Name in this reality) is a combination of the words, **He was, He is, He will be, and He makes everything be.**

Time is a creation that God made. He is not in time.

Let's try to crystallize this difficult thought. Imagine you were looking at a map of the world but there was a large sheet of paper with a hole covering the map. Through the peep hole you could see one country at a time. As you moved the sheet of paper from west to east you begin to see other countries and continents; you go from America to Europe to Asia all in a continuous time sequence. Now imagine if you just removed the paper entirely, you would then be able to see the whole map at once.

As far as we can understand, the Omniscient One sees the past and future **in the present**, since He clearly transcends time. If so, we can say that the Almighty knows what we are going to do **because from His perspective we have already done it!**

Now however we get a handle on this mind boggling idea, the bottom line is that God knows what we will do in the future, but in such a way, that it does not affect our ability to choose freely.

"Wait a minute," you may protest. "I can accept that God's foreknowledge somehow doesn't obligate me to act in a certain way but if He **decreed** that I act in a certain way then that would definitely obligate me." So let's try and understand this very intriguing concept.

Foreknowledge Used to Bring Out a Plan and yet Maintain Our Free-will

Although God's foreknowledge doesn't obligate us, **God does use His foreknowledge to bring out certain decrees.** So in the case of the Egyptian servitude, God saw the future and saw that some Egyptians would freely choose to subjugate the Jews. He therefore decreed that the Jewish enslavement would happen in Egypt where He knew that some Egyptians would freely choose to subjugate them.

In this way people have free-will and God's plan is implemented.

In fact, there is a very amazing model to understand how these "matches" are made in the beginning of time and yet we have free-will. You see it's absurd to think that you choose to do something and then the Omnipotent One needs to scramble to find the appropriate response and conduit. If it was decreed that Sam should be killed by Paul and Paul decides to become righteous and not to kill, do you imagine that God has to quickly go out and look for other takers who are willing to do the job? Certainly not. Rather, all possible choices for every act and every response are already pre-hardwired into the fabric of reality like branches that extend from a tree. When you choose a certain pathway all the possible routes and ramifications for that system open up while the other possible courses are closed down.

Let's now apply this understanding to the decree of servitude in Egypt.

God tells Avraham, "Know that your children will be strangers in a land not their own, and they will be subjugated and tormented for four hundred years." It turns out that Egypt is the place where the Jews were subjugated and finally redeemed in the amazing way the text describes. However, there is a problem with the historical calculation. If you compute how many years the Jews were actually in Egypt, it was only 210 years! So why does the verse say we will be strangers for 400 years?

The Talmud tells us not to be concerned over the apparent missing 190 years. The text didn't specifically say Egypt; it said that Avraham's children would be strangers in a land not their own for 400 years. If you calculate the time when Avraham's child Yitzchak (Isaac) is born, who himself was a stranger in the land of Israel (as the Jews were not given ownership of Israel until after they were redeemed from Egypt) until Yitzchak's descendants go down to Egypt, you will find it is exactly 190 years! So the 400 years of strangers and servitude refers to 190 years of strangers in Israel without ownership and 210 more years of the Egyptian servitude.

Nonetheless, if you read the text simply it could definitely mean that the Jews will be in Egyptian servitude for 400 years. And the reason why the text also contains that meaning is *because that scenario was also possible*. Since the decree is combined with free-will choices, there are various ways that the plan can come to fruition. The mystics teach that if the Jews could have maintained their spiritual level throughout all 400 years of Egyptian servitude, the reality would be expressed through *that* pathway **and the Jewish people would suffer no more exiles.** Unfortunately, the Jews in Egypt fell to the lowest spiritual level, called the 49th level of impurity. If they would have remained one more moment in Egypt, they would have become so absorbed into the degenerate Egyptian society that they would no longer have been redeemed as Jews. To accomplish the grand plan, the Almighty extricated them exactly after 210 years so they would not be lost in Egypt.

Did our free-will *force* the Almighty to quickly look for an alternative route to fulfill the 400-year decree? Not at all. The 400-year decree was woven into the fabric of history from the outset in other possible ways. These different pathways can be invoked based on our choices. And so when the Jewish nation chose to sink to the lowest level in Egypt, the pathway of the 400-year decree was enacted from the birth of Yitzchak. However, according to this pathway, the Jewish nation had not completed the challenges they needed to face over 400 years worth of slavery in Egypt. The extreme challenges of the remaining 190 years would now be expressed in the form of the later Jewish exiles from the Holy land. **An alternative pathway was followed based on our free-will decision even though the potential for that choice was always there.**

Let's review what we have said so far.

1. Free-will is essential for the purpose of creation as we discussed in chapters one and three.

2. God uses people's free-will choices to accomplish His grand plan whether they choose to act positively or negatively.

3. God will match people who choose to act in a certain way with people who need to receive that act.

4. Although God knows what we will choose that does not force us to act in any way.

5. The Omniscient One may use His knowledge of the future to align people and events while still leaving them their free-will to choose.

Okay, we have solved our dilemma on one level. As if this chapter is not confusing enough, let's now make our problem just a little stickier.

Free-will Even When You Are Decreed

We have a tradition that a person is judged on Rosh Hashanah (the New Year) as to what will happen to him or her during the year. However, this doesn't mean everything is completely locked in and predetermined. Everyone is additionally judged at every second, and so, in certain circumstances, people can change the Rosh Hashanah decree. Let's now revisit our poor friend Sam who has been having a tough time in our examples and imagine that it is decreed on Rosh Hashanah that he will die during the year, unless he can have the decree changed for some reason. If we further examine the details of Sam's "death sentence" we find that Paul is the one who is destined to kill him. Now let's pretend that somehow Paul "finds out" that he is meant to kill Sam. Paul now has a much greater complaint for the Heavenly complaint department. When Paul is being judged in the Heavenly Court he will plead innocence because he can claim, **I did what I was supposed to do.** I was specifically decreed to kill Sam and I was only doing the Divine will. I was incapable of passing the job to someone else since I was singled out for the task. Accordingly, Paul seems to be entitled to reward instead of punishment. So how in the world can we hold Paul culpable for his deeds?

Our Sages reveal a very interesting approach in which *thought* actually determines the import of action. Imagine a scene where Sam is speeding down the road wildly and cuts Paul off. Paul is irate and in his anger he chases after Sam who just keeps racing along. Paul cannot believe Sam's reckless driving. Paul's rage begins to build inside of him. Paul screams at Sam but Sam is preoccupied and ignores him. Finally, Paul, who is an angry, violent person in the first place, pulls out a gun and shoots Sam dead. In this scenario Paul is a murderer and will be judged accordingly.

Now imagine the same scene except in this version Paul is paying closer attention to Sam's actions as Sam races down the road. Paul now notices why Sam is driving so quickly. Sam is actually chasing a person in the car in front of him with the intention of shooting him dead. Paul sees that Sam has in fact cocked his gun and he is taking aim at this innocent person. There is no way that Paul can prevent this murder without shooting Sam. Jewish law states that if someone is going to kill someone else and there is no way to prevent it other than by killing the potential murderer first, you must save the innocent life by killing the pursuer. Paul recognizes that this is the situation and he shoots Sam, thereby saving the potential victim.

Is Paul guilty of murder in this case? Of course not. He acted in a righteous way in accordance with the law. So what is really the difference between the two cases? There is only one essential difference: Paul's intent is different in these two situations. **In both scenarios Paul has been chosen to be the conduit to kill Sam but the morality of the act is completely altered based on Paul's intentions.**

This approach can be understood through the actions of the evil Babylonian King Nebuchadnezzar. Nebuchadnezzar was a very vile human being and one of his evil deeds was the killing and exiling of the Jewish people. Now we know that Nebuchadnezzar is held accountable for these actions. Yet if you read the Book of Jeremiah (in Hebrew, Yirmiyahu), you will see that Yirmiyahu not only prophesized about the upcoming destruction of Israel but he even named the man who would do it, Nebuchadnezzar! Imagine Nebuchadnezzar reading the local newspaper one day and the headlines read, "Yirmiyahu Prophesizes Nebuchadnezzar to Destroy Jerusalem." Nebuchadnezzar's attorney could certainly claim her client is innocent since Nebuchadnezzar was just fulfilling the word of God. He was doing as the Prophet said and this was recorded for all to see.

No such luck for Nebuchadnezzar, though. Our response to his lawyer is: it is true that if Nebuchadnezzar was functioning like a court emissary that delivers the lethal injection to the convict on death row he would not have transgressed the law, but if someone enters the prison and kills the accused for his own purposes, he too is a murderer. And even if the court emissary himself kills the convict over some disagreement they had five minutes before the execution time, he is no longer functioning as a messenger of the court and is guilty. (2*)

The upshot of this approach can obviously be extremely deranged and misguided. There are certainly enough cases in the world of fanatics who are convinced that they are doing the "Creators will" and allow themselves to commit the most heinous crimes against humanity. Still, if someone really did know what the Divine will was and acted for that reason, then their actions would be positive. A parent who disciplines a child to train him is different than a stranger who yells at someone because of anger. The intent of the individual can change the moral import of the act 180 degrees.

Free to Choose but the Plan Still Happens

Let me share another analogy to explain how an Omnipotent Director guides the world with a cosmic plan and yet people have free-will.

Picture a town where the governor wants to improve the local economy. He takes a giant plot of land and divides it into three sections. He assigns three different individuals with the task of developing the land. Their job is to increase their wealth and in turn the wealth of the town. Bachelor number 1 decides to plant a variety of crops on his lot and he transforms the land into a successful farm. Bachelor number 2 decides to raise cattle and uses his land for grazing and raising various types of animals. Bachelor number 3 is lazy. He doesn't like to work at all, certainly doesn't want to be told what to do, and has no interest in making use of the section he was given. He spends his time intentionally trashing his land. He takes a pickax and hacks the land, destroying everything in his sight and making numerous holes and ditches throughout the beautiful land.

If the governor was an Omnipotent Being, he would be able to accomplish his objective of improving the economy even while allowing Bachelor number 3 to do whatever he wanted. For example, Bachelor number 3 hacks at the land, and discovers an oil well beneath the ground. Or his "hacking" actually improves the soil and causes seeds to sprout prolifically. Bachelor number 3, with all his bad intentions, can unwittingly strike oil and help improve the town's economy, just as the governor wanted. Unfortunately, this Bachelor will obviously be punished for his negligent intentions *even though the act produced the positive result the governor wanted.*

So even in the most extreme case where a person's actions may be determined (like in Nebuchadnezzar's case), still the freedom to choose *the intent* of the action changes the action itself. All of these approaches are crucial to understand because it is a principle in life: God directs the world to its purpose and yet people have free-will. Accordingly, you may ask, if free-will is so central to all of existence, is it ever possible that someone can lose their free-will?

The answer is yes, it is possible.

What? Doesn't that contradict everything we have been saying?

When Free-Will Is Removed

Let's investigate the archetypal case in the Torah and see if we can figure this one out. The classic case that everyone points to is the account of Pharaoh in Egypt. God brings plagues upon Pharaoh and Egypt and orders him to set the Jews free. Yet Pharaoh refuses to heed God's demands; he consistently hardens his heart and continues to enslave the Jews. At a crucial juncture, after the fifth plague, the Torah no longer says that Pharaoh hardened his *own* heart but rather that "**God** hardened Pharaoh's heart." Moses (in Hebrew, Moshe) is even made privy to the fact that there is no longer any chance that Pharaoh will release the Jews until all the ten plagues are completed.

But if that is so, then Pharaoh actually has no free-will left. He can no longer make decisions that are of moral import. How can that possibly be? Haven't we already posited that the power of free-will is the fundamental ingredient to the entire purpose of the world? (3*)

Listen carefully to this approach. There is a phenomenon that sometimes occurs in the world where a person's prior actions lock them into a set way of acting in the future. This is usually the result of a person getting stuck in habits and becoming psychologically adapted to a certain way of thinking and acting. This type of *entrapment* is not absolute. However, there can also be an exceptional situation where a person is *trapped* in a way of acting as a **consequence and punishment** for his or her earlier actions. This was the case with Pharaoh. Since Pharaoh consistently hardened his heart and refused to free the Jews, God removed his free-will to act otherwise. Now Pharaoh **was just a pawn being used to demonstrate a lesson for the entire world.** This is what God reveals to Moshe. He is now keeping Pharaoh alive to show God's complete mastery and providence in the world. This is the lesson we learn from the Egyptian redemption.

"Hold on a minute!" you exclaim. "This still doesn't answer our question. How can Pharaoh be held accountable for his actions when he is not free to choose otherwise?" The answer is that Pharaoh is not held accountable for those actions; he is held accountable for the actions that preceded the removal of his free-will and that led to its removal! In this sense Pharaoh is actually no longer alive. He is just a walking dead man. He has already been judged for his acts and is now being used as an instrument to bring out the grand plan, irrespective of his individual wishes. (4*)

Everything That Happens Fits into the System

All of this leads to the vital melding of two seemingly disparate concepts. On the one hand, every person receives exactly what they are supposed to get. The events or circumstances of our lives happen to us for a myriad of reasons. These reasons include: being challenged to grow (Chapter Three); being part of our unique mission (Chapter Two); being a result of our actions (Chapter Six), etc.

Simultaneously, though, every event is crafted to fit exactly into God's grand plan to bring the world to perfection. If people act properly, perfection will be attained with positive responses. If people act negatively, perfection may be brought about through negative means.

Either way the system works. This is what the Jewish mystics call the Providence of Judgment *(Hanhagat HaMishpat)* and the Providence of Unity *(Hanhagat HaYichud)*. We have free-will, we decide how to act and there are consequences to our actions; **yet the Omnipotent One aligns everything so it all leads to completion.**

Consequently, there is an amazing life changing rule that emerges from this. Nobody can do anything to you that should not happen. No one can take anything from you that you are supposed to have. No one can harm you in a way that is not meant to be part of a greater purpose.

This maxim is evident in an amazing Jewish law that forbids revenge or bearing a grudge. Revenge is when you retaliate against someone for something that they did against you. If you won't lend your ax to someone because they didn't lend you their hammer, that is called revenge. On the other hand, if you agree to lend them your ax but you angrily say, "I will lend you my ax because I'm not like you," that is called bearing a grudge. Both acts are prohibited in Jewish law.

Now we can understand that it would be very noble not to be vengeful or grudge bearing, but how can a person possibly avoid such natural human emotions? There is one way to successfully accomplish this. We can incorporate into our consciousness the idea that everything that happens to us is a message from the Omnipotent Source and no one can affect us otherwise. So if you are not given that hammer by your neighbor there is no point in getting angry at the "pawn" - he's just delivering the message. It's true that he may be a "bad guy" and even a conduit for "bad things" but **that is his problem not yours.**

There is a reason you should not get a hammer now; maybe it's to teach you a lesson about your own selfishness, maybe it's a repayment for something you didn't do for a friend, maybe you were going to smash your finger with the hammer because you're a klutz. We don't know the exact reason, but whatever it is, there is a deeper meaning why this happened to you now. We can stop and think about that.

The analogy is to the proverbial dumb dog. Though I'm sure you may know of a dog who is incredibly smart, still, you've certainly seen dogs that aren't the brightest of canines. Imagine witnessing someone throwing a stick at a dog that hits him smack in the head. What does a dumb dog do? The dumb dog gets really angry and violently starts biting the stick. That is obviously foolish. The stick didn't do anything; it was just the tool of the guy who threw it.

But this is exactly the same with us. Although a free-will person who harms us is certainly culpable and will have to pay for what he has done, nonetheless, he is nothing more than a stick, the way we saw that Yosef's brothers were only the agents for getting Yosef to Egypt.

"If so," you may reply, "I should be angry at the source, the one who threw the stick." According to what we've said, that is God.

Sometimes we feel angry at God and think things are not fair. What we need to realize is that the Omnipotent One has a just, accurate, and precise reason why He lets these things happen to us, even if it's beyond what we can fathom right now.

The really good news I want to share with you is that God is not only doing what is correct but He is also directing things in our best interest and for our ultimate good. We will explore this important subject in the next chapter.

Application One:

Think about someone that hurt you in your life. Notice the negative emotions that arise inside of you. Now manipulate your recollection of this person to make them non-threatening, foolish, pathetic or comical. Accomplish this by altering something about them in your mind, for example, make their voice squeaky, make them look like a cartoon character, or exaggerate one of their features, etc. For a few moments, see, hear and/or feel this new impression in your mind's eye.

Now think about the event that hurt you. Tell yourself that the person acting negatively towards you was just a "pawn messenger" and that the situation needed to happen for a deeper reason. The individual that hurt you was insignificant since what happened would have happened to you anyway; with or without that particular person. The fact that this individual chose to be the negative stick is their problem, *not yours!* In a certain way the person is a conduit for your growth even though they didn't want to be.

In this very difficult exercise, you will need to allow these emotions to stir inside you a while and then create a phrase that will encapsulate the message for you. For example, say the phrase "no one can take what is meant for me" or "he or she were just pawns in my journey" or any adage that resonates this concept to you. Repeat the adage to yourself, making the voice in your head louder and/or more persuasive.

Now we will attempt to transform the emotion to sympathy. If you are not able to develop sympathy for this person who was a negative sore in your life, do not worry; simply going through this process will help you solidify greater indifference to them, which is also a positive step.

See if you can identify one good trait about your antagonist. Now meditate on that aspect of good in them. Most people are not completely evil so it is easier than you think. After you have clearly celebrated one positive aspect of this person you can wonder to yourself, "if they have this positive feature how could they have been so bad to me?" Quickly answer your question: *because in regards to this issue with me*

they are blind, undeveloped or unschooled. Realize that their inability to act properly towards you is *their* shortcoming. Accept the axiom, "what a poor, unknowing individual they must be if they can't even realize how badly they act."

That really is not your problem though. You are going to take what you need to grow and maybe someday this person will mature to see the truth. You may even hope or pray that they do develop understanding, but it is really not your issue; you are no longer doing the dance with them.

Now you may say to yourself, "who am I to say this person is blind or undeveloped?" In life you need to make decisions on how you see the world. So ask yourself, "is there any aspect of what this person did against me that was justified? Is there any lesson I need to learn from what happened? Is there any way I could have acted better?"

Realize that in most situations no one is 100% right while the other is 100% wrong. So even if you are 90% right, take the responsibility for the 10% you were mistaken in. Learn from that how you can act better in the future. If you do this, then you have really made this person a conduit for your growth and no longer need to bear a grudge against them. We don't know if they will ever acknowledge the 90% that they were wrong, but either way, that is not our problem.

You are now able to move on with your journey and deal directly with the Omnipotent Source Who really does guide your life.

Endnotes

(1*) I write "sometimes" because there are actually two different types of soul mates. The "first match" called Zivug Rishon is prearranged in the Heavens and is, so to speak, the other half of your soul from its inception. This does not require redirecting or re-aligning anything as the match was already made before time. If each of the pair follows their destiny and becomes what they should be, they will meet and become a couple.

However, since both parties have free-will and can become whatever they want, they may end up deserving a different soul mate than was originally destined. Imagine a scenario where one of the pair becomes tremendously righteous and the other one becomes exceedingly evil. They would obviously no longer be appropriate for each other.

At that point, each one of the couple would move from the system of the "first match," Zivug Rishon, to the system of the "second match" called the Zivug Sheni. The Zivug Sheni is determined by what you become through your deeds. Based on the personality and character one develops, one will be entitled to a soul mate appropriate to the person they are now. However, when a couple moves to a Zivug Sheni system there is a tremendous rearranging of reality that is required. The couple is now being re-paired with people who also had "first matches" (Zivug Rishon) and so there is a chain reaction of situations that have to be brought together. The Zivug Sheni requires turning the world upside down and is therefore painted as something difficult to do. (This is a figurative term because for the Omnipotent One there cannot be anything "difficult.")

(2*) There is another resolution to this issue that I have not included in the main text because it is easily misunderstood. It also can obfuscate the conclusions of this chapter if not comprehended clearly. For the sake of thoroughness, I am including it here. The Omnipotent One may sometimes choose to "leave room" in the decree for a human being to act beyond what is decreed. There was a decree against the Jews that was destined to come through Nebuchadnezzar but there was an added part that God "allowed" Nebuchadnezzar to further subjugate and persecute the Jews more than was decreed, if he chose to do so. That part was not dictated; it could and should have been avoided by Nebuchadnezzar. However, Nebuchadnezzar crossed the line and that is what he was punished for.

Similarly, on Rosh Hashanah, if someone is decreed to be killed, two different scenarios can occur. In one scenario it can be ordained that someone will have a fracas with a hardened killer, a person that kills without hesitation. The judgment then is certain death. Alternatively, a person can be placed in the hands of someone that is challenged on those free-will battle lines and will not obviously murder someone in such a case. If the potential murderer goes forward and kills someone, then that was one side of the victim's decree and that judgment is itself the rectification of the victim. On the other hand, if the potential killer decides not to kill, he has made a great sanctification in the world and since the potential victim was the vehicle for that, a rectification is also gained by our potential victim.

We see this unique power of human action affecting others in the story of Yosef that is recorded in Genesis. When Reuven, the eldest brother, implored the brothers not to kill Yosef, he suggested that they throw Yosef in a pit filled with snakes and scorpions instead; a situation that may well have killed him anyway. But Reuven understood that if Yosef did not deserve to die, the animals would not be able to harm Yosef.

However, in certain cases a person may succeed in killing another even if it is not fully decreed. This is because the merit required to stop the actions of a free-will human being are so great that maybe Yosef would not be worthy of that kind of protection.

God prefers not to control people's area of freedom and so a human being's actions are rarely stopped and he is sometimes even given the ability to "add" to a decree. Still, as in the Rosh Hashanah example above, it is not a free for all. The judgment is specific even for the one placed into the hands of the "uncertain killer." The person deserves and is judged to specifically be put in the position where a human being will make a far-reaching decision towards them. The decision made by the individual will accomplish the goals either way. Similarly, the Jews at the time of the Babylonian destruction were delivered into Nebuchadnezzar's hand. When he chose to persecute them more than required, that provided the atonement the Jews needed for their actions. If he would have chosen not to additionally persecute them, his positive decision would have impacted the world and the Jews in a way that would have also brought them their rectification. Nebuchadnezzar himself is punished for choosing the negative rectification when he could have chosen the positive one.

(3) Note the difference between this type of freedom and what we discussed in
Chapter Two. In Chapter Two we explained that certain circumstances in
life may be predetermined; i.e., if a person is rich or poor, strong or weak,
etc. This does not contradict free-will because there is no limitation on the
person's moral freedom. They are free to act righteously regardless of their
life circumstances. Here, however, if God is hardening Pharaoh's heart
not to free the Jews that is forcing him to act in a way that is morally
depraved.*

(4) Another approach to explain why God would harden Pharaoh's heart if
that removes free-will can be understood by our discussion in Chapter
Three. In that chapter we demonstrated that in order to have free-will,
reality needs to be somewhat concealed so that there is room to delude
ourselves. If God revealed Himself in a completely obvious way, it would
be impossible to do anything counter to that understanding. Since God
performed these incredible miracles of the ten plagues, Pharaoh's free-
will to do anything against God had been compromised. The truth was
so apparent that any normal human being would certainly free the Jews
after seeing these wonders. Consequently, God hardened Pharaoh's heart
proportionately to the marvels Pharaoh had witnessed. This restored the
balance of Pharaoh's free-will and allowed him to again choose for himself.*

CHAPTER FIVE

HAPPINESS AND THE EXPERIENCE OF EVIL

Imagine you had some personal force that protected you so that no harm could befall you. How would that make you feel?

To understand the emotion that is produced by such an experience we must reveal a principle that our Sages teach us. They tell us that similar sounding words in Hebrew, i.e., homonyms, also have connected meanings. The experience of being able to trust or rely on someone thoroughly is called in Hebrew *"lesmoch."* It is therefore very significant that the word *"lesmoch"* also means "to be happy." There is an obvious correlation between feeling that you can truly rely on someone and a secure sense of happiness. But who can you possibly rely on so thoroughly? Who has the power to really protect you in all situations?

Although being able to rely on friends and family does make us feel good, their ability to help us is obviously significantly limited. To create that complete sense of security, the power would need to be omnipotent. So the million-dollar question is: what do we call that omnipotent force? If you answered God, you are correct and can move on to double jeopardy.

One Source for Good and Evil

We have one serious problem though. Can we honestly believe that God protects us from all harm? Many people who believe in God only relate to Him from an attitude that illustrates the motto "please don't hurt me." Their concept of God is of a vengeful Being, and, at least subconsciously, they feel that if He would just leave them alone and not punish them, things would be okay.

Even if that isn't your perspective, we need to honestly ask how we can genuinely feel trust and protected in a world with so much tragedy. The world is a scary place with a lot of suffering and difficulty, so how and why can we believe that an Omnipotent Being will shield us?

This dilemma is actually at the heart of many religious and philosophical systems. Man has struggled throughout the ages to reconcile a vision of a benevolent Omnipotent Being with a world where evil exists. The Zoroastrians had invented two gods, one of good and light, the other of evil and darkness, and although that may seem bizarre to us, if we appreciate the contradiction of good and evil in the world, we can at least understand where they were coming from. This same enigma plagues us in the modern day.

A student of mine who became a Rabbi in a southern state in America was driving to work his first week on the job and decided to hear what the religious pulse was in the town. He turned on the radio and tuned into a religious talk show. He heard an aggrieved man call in and ask the preacher, "Why is there so much suffering and pain in this world?"

He complained to the preacher saying, "It just isn't right!" The preacher's response to the pained caller was very telling. He rebuffed the caller and told him that this issue is only a problem if you're a Jew! "Because if you are a Jew you believe it's all from God but we believe that the devil did it!"

My point of telling this story is not to belittle the preacher; from his perspective this makes sense. He can resolve this conflict of good and evil by attributing power to an entity of evil. However, from a Jewish perspective, we declare that everything emanates from God. If we would invest anything in the world with a power to 'fight' God's will, even in the slightest way, we would breach the fundamental Jewish commandment against idolatry. We affirm that God is completely Benevolent, Omnipotent and He is One in all possible Oneness; there can be no other power. We don't believe in a "separate" powerful devil. And that is precisely the problem. Since no created being can diverge from His will, how can there be evil? And being that we see evil in this world, how can we possibly rely on this Omnipotent Source and feel completely protected?

A Personality That Sees Good Even When It Appears Negative

Let's start by painting a biographical sketch of a person who embodies complete confidence in this Omnipotent Being. From there we will be able to unravel our philosophical dilemma. Many human beings have successfully developed tremendous trust in the Almighty that is even hard to fathom. The Jewish patriarch Avraham (who was actually the father of numerous great nations), was able to bring his dearest son, Yitzchak, as a potential offering because he trusted so thoroughly. Many of Avraham's descendants followed along a similar path. And there was one of the Sages in Talmudic times who mastered this level of trust so thoroughly that it became his trademark nickname, *Nachum Ish Gam Zu.*

This Sage's first name was just Nachum but he had been given the appellation of *Ish Gam Zu* which means "the man of this also." One explanation of the origin of this strange appellation was based on a phrase that Nachum would constantly repeat. Whatever would happen to Nachum, good, bad or ugly, he would remark, "*Gam zu le tova*," which means "this is also for the good." Hence they called him Nachum, "the man of this also is for the good." The other great Sages in Nachum's time were so impressed with his approach to life that they believed God dealt with Nachum in a supernatural manner, so much so that when the Roman occupiers of Israel were looking for a pretense to increase their tyrannical decrees against the Jews, the Sages felt the best person to represent the Jewish people would be Nachum Ish Gam Zu.

According to the account in the Talmud, Nachum was sent from Israel to Rome with a giant coffer filled with gold, silver, diamonds and jewels to present to the Roman Emperor as a gift before making his plea for the Jewish people. Nachum took this chest of treasure and began the trip to Rome. Along the way he stopped at an inn and stayed overnight. While he was sleeping, the inn keeper and his cohorts stole the chest and its contents. They removed the riches and re-filled the chest with earth, to prevent their thievery from being discovered. When Nachum arose in the morning, he took his treasure chest and continued on his way to Rome.

At the entrance to the palace of the Emperor, Nachum Ish Gam Zu was ushered into the waiting hall to await the opportunity to speak with the Emperor.

When the Emperor's official announced the arrival of the Jewish emissary from Israel, Nachum entered bearing the gift of the Jews. The "treasure chest" was opened and upon seeing the mounds of earth offered to the Emperor by his Jewish subjects he became outraged and declared, "Off with his head, kill the messenger and the Jews will also receive what is due them!!"

Now imagine what would we say if we were Nachum Ish Gam Zu at that treacherous moment? When I ask that question in a lecture most people just say, "Rabbi, what I would say I can't repeat in front of you!"

Well, whatever you would have said, I can assure you that Nachum didn't say that; all he said was, *"Gam zu le tova* - this is also for good."

At that moment, one of the king's officers came before the King and suggested that maybe this earth was some kind of magical dirt (the Romans were quite superstitious). "Your majesty, it is not like the Jews to be so insolent. Perhaps the Jews have sent you this supernatural gift with special power to help your Highness."

Immediately, the Emperor sent off this treasure chest of earth to the front lines of a battle they were losing. They tried this earth and were able to defeat their enemy and win the battle (1*). Word was sent back to the Emperor that the earth was in fact magical. Not only was Nachum's life spared but the Emperor filled the chest with jewels and riches of his own. He sent this as a reward to express his gratitude to the Jews for their wonderful gift.

On the return trip to Israel, Nachum stayed in the same inn. The innkeeper couldn't believe his eyes. Hadn't he replaced the jewels with dirt? How could the Emperor have repaid Nachum Ish Gam Zu with such honor for bringing dirt?!

Finally, he approached Nachum and asked him, "What was it that you brought the Emperor that warranted such an honorable reward"?

Nachum replied, "What I took from here is what I delivered there."

The innkeeper thought he was literally sitting on a gold mine, so he packed up a chest of dirt and brought it to the Emperor. "The magical dirt of Nachum Ish Gam Zu came from my home!" he announced heartily. The Emperor graciously accepted the gift and had the earth tested to see if it also contained the miraculous powers. When the test failed the innkeeper was executed the way the Emperor had originally planned to kill Nachum Ish Gam Zu.

Is Seeing the Good in Every Circumstance Appropriate?

Now this is certainly a wonderful story, but it behooves us to deliberate if Nachum's approach to life is good or not? Is this a realistic and healthy way to see the world, or is it a naïve, Pollyanna approach to existence? Nachum seems to float through life with a sense of complete trust in God. Though this may provide a feeling of serenity, it seems a bit absurd and somewhat dangerous. Is this what the Almighty expects or wants from us?

Furthermore, in Nachum's world it almost seems like there is no evil. His response to everything that looks bad is simply, "it is also for good." Yet if that is true, why does Jewish Law obligate one type of blessing for good things that occur and a completely different blessing for when bad things occur? Upon a good occurrence a person blesses *Hatov vehametiv*, that God is good and bestows goodness; conversely, if something negative happens, a person makes the blessing, *Dayan Haemes*, stating that God is a True Judge.

According to Nachum though, since everything is for the good, a person should always make the blessing *Hatov vehametiv*, that God bestows good upon us, because it's all good! The blessing on evil should not even exist since in his view there really is no evil!

Synthesizing the Emotional Experience with the Intellectual Understanding

To understand this dichotomy, we must realize that there are different levels of human experience. On an emotional level, a person's response to good things is the complete opposite of his response to bad things. **This is not only natural but it is essential for a human being**. If a person would respond to a death with a cold dispassionate statement, "well, it's all for good," we'd consider him in denial or not in touch with his true feelings. In spiritual terms, not to cry over the death of a good person is considered cruel. Consequently, the Talmud says that a person is rewarded when visiting a house of mourning specifically for his or her silence and compassion. The responsibility of the comforting visitors is to listen, thereby expressing empathy and sympathy with the mourner's pain. Anyone who tries to intellectualize the pain away is considered a negative fool. This is the heart level which is required of us in order to be whole. As human beings we need to be able to experience the entire emotional spectrum.

However, there is another level, which is the intellectual dimension. Beyond the emotional sadness experienced through a negative event, there is a tempered state where there is knowledge that somehow, in someway, the Omnipotent One moves everything to "good." The blessing, *Dayan Haemes*, God is a True Judge, expresses the concept that although we may not feel good about what has occurred, we acknowledge that the Omnipotent One is doing what is right and true. In that spirit we can intellectually recognize that it may be part of a greater plan for good that we just can't comprehend at the present moment. Nachum Ish Gam Zu had developed this confidence in God so thoroughly that he clearly knew all negative things were actually for a positive outcome. This awareness was so inculcated into his being that he was even emotionally able to perceive *gam zu le tova*, it is all for the good, in every situation.

This same rationale is behind one of the Torah's prohibitions, forbidding people to cut or mutilate themselves when a loved one dies. The nations of the world had such a practice and the Torah forbade it. The Torah concludes this commandment against self-mutilation for a loss by saying, "You are children of God." But what is the connection between prohibiting mutilation and being children of God?

The connection is that although mourning and crying are necessary and appropriate in such a sad situation, excessive mourning to the point of inflicting wounds is only possible if death is viewed as the complete cessation of existence. If the loved one who died is totally lost and gone forever, maybe we could justify such behavior. However, if we are children of God and the soul returns to the Almighty and is only lost to us for the moment, the pain is somewhat mitigated. This idea obviates the rational for such mutilation. Death is certainly sad and must be mourned on the emotional level. Yet on the intellectual level there is the understanding that a benevolent Creator is directing the world and every part of it for the good; including even the most heartbreaking tragedies.

Expanding Our Vision with the Possibility That Negative Things Can Be for the Good

"Wait a minute," you exclaim. "Why should I believe that this Creator is moving everything towards the good? I don't see that in my life and can't even dream of a way that horrific things can turn out for the best."

Fair enough. So let's try to expand our vision with an analogy that will allow us to probe the inner depths of this concept. Imagine for a moment that you saw a masked man with a knife moving towards his victim with the intention of chopping his leg off. You see this horrible scene and you quickly jump in front of the masked man and scream, "Stop! Get out of here."

The masked man looks at you with disbelief and says, "Sir, do you know where you are? This is an operating room and that man has gangrene. If we don't amputate his leg immediately he will die!"

"Oh," you bashfully excuse yourself, "I'm sorry, please ignore me. Sorry to interfere!"

What happened in this scenario? You saw part of a scene and drew a certain conclusion. Yet if you would have seen the entire picture, you would have drawn the opposite conclusion; **the apparently evil act of cutting off someone's leg was actually a kind act to save his life.**

This concept is born out in an amazing way from the Hebrew word for evil, *ra* - רַע. Although *ra* is generally translated as evil, that isn't the literal meaning of the word. To understand the etymology of the word let's look at what happens in the synagogue during High Holiday services. On Rosh Hashanah we blow the shofar in a sequence of three different sounds. One sound we make is called the *Teruah* - תרעה. The *Teruah* sound is a repetitive broken, fragmented sound. When we look at the word *Teruah* - תרעה, we notice that the root of the word is *Ra*, which means evil. What can possibly be the connection between a broken, fragmented sound and the concept of evil?

The connection is a startling and amazing lesson: **our experience of evil (*ra*) is a result of our limited perspective.**

We are only capable of seeing a partial and fragmented reality. However, if we were able to perceive the grander perspective we would discern that *ra* - evil - is actually used as a vehicle for good! In our example of the surgeon amputating the patient's leg, the observer was only witnessing a fragment of the whole picture. Therefore, the observer was only able to perceive the act as cruel and horrible. However, once the observer was able to see the entire picture, he understood that the apparent cruelty was actually an act of kindness.

This concept represents a very deep understanding of the world. The *Kabbalists* explain that the whole purpose of creating evil was to accentuate and truly experience the ultimate good. Let's exert our brains and try to comprehend this very deep and philosophical thought.

The greatest pleasure we can have is to experience the Infinite. In other words: to experience God. We are hardwired in such a way that we have some means to grasp the Infinite One. Yet if we try to comprehend how the Infinite One reveals Himself based on what He is, we will realize that we have no access. For example, try to understand God's infinite kindness. What can we say? God's kindness is really, really, *really* kind.

How can we perceive the Infinite?

What we can have some handle on is the idea that He is One, since this is predicated on understanding **what He is *not*.** He is not limited in any way. There is no other power, force, or independent existence other than Him.

In order to perceive this truth, we were created to live in a reality where we can think other people or events dictate our lives. We feel that our leaders, our bosses, or happenstance are all factors in our lives.

Imagine we have a boss that is ruining our life with his sarcasm and unreasonable demands. At the outset of the relationship we cower before him because we are threatened by his power. Is our fear simply our boss' fault or does it signify a shortcoming in us? If we were confident with our abilities, assured of our employment value, and undaunted by aggression, wouldn't we relate differently to our boss? As time goes on though, we are forced to face our weaknesses and eventually learn how to stand up to our boss. In retrospect, was it not our "evil" boss that was the catalyst that triggered our newfound strength and self-respect?

Now let's expand this concept to a global level. What is the source of our delusion that there are other powers in the world?

As we discussed earlier in Chapter Three, the Infinite One concealed His light and His complete omnipotence to create this reality. This concealment is the root of all negativity. The system of negativity (evil) is then structured from that concealment. Therefore, when the concealment/evil is removed we are able to experience that Infinite light. As a matter of fact, we can say that the great revelation of Oneness is because **evil exists in the first place to remove!**

In this way, evil is a kind of illusion. It is borne out of concealment and causes us to struggle in various ways to see through the veil. Eventually, the experience of trying to see in the dark strengthens our sight and when the light is revealed, our vision is clearer than it would have been before the dark.

In essence, ***the darkness has specifically added to the experience of light***.

This is the meaning of the verse in Psalms that discusses the eventual return to Zion after our long and arduous exile. The verse says, "When God will return the exiles to Zion, it will be like we were dreamers." How could it be that our real pain in exile can be compared to dreaming?

As history unfolds, we experientially begin to see how the Omnipotent One is directing all things towards His grand plan. This culminates with the visceral knowledge that all the suffering, difficulty and pain in our lives was purposeful and for a greater plan. Just like in our example of the "evil" boss who ultimately makes us stronger and clearer, the eventual revelation that nothing was arbitrary and out of control throughout history will generate tremendous clarity on the deepest level. It will make the prelude of our existence in times of concealment feel exactly like a dream. The pains of exile will all make sense to us in our new waking state. At that moment we will understand in our bones that there is no other source, no other power and nothing random in the world, rather only One, the Almighty. We can then fully *experience* Oneness, our handle to experiencing the Divine.

Although this is an extremely lofty idea, we can all relate to this in our own terms. Every one of us can look back at some events in our lives that were extremely painful when we were going through them. At the time, we would have given anything to get out of the situation we were in. Yet with the benefit of hindsight, many times when we analyze it in the present, we realize that often it was those specific situations that made us what we are today.

For example, let's say we had the traumatic experience of being bullied in school. During the time that this was happening, we hated going to school and our difficult, painful circumstances. However, years later we became a crusader for human rights and dignity. We were compelled and empowered to stand up for justice in the world. And what inspired us to become such a strong, devoted, sensitive person? It may be precisely because of the negative experiences we went through in our school years. In hindsight, we appreciate what we gained from that negative experience.

On the emotional level, the elation that arises after sorrow is also significant. Imagine the joy and security we would feel if we had five million dollars in the bank. Now imagine how we would feel if we thought that we lost all that money in some investment scam. In the midst of the anguish, we discover that the money we lost was actually deposited into some other investment and had in fact doubled. We now own ten million dollars when we thought we had nothing! Not only has our money doubled but so has our euphoria. That is the benefit, the purpose of sorrow. It is precisely the pain of darkness that can lead to the greater clarity and joy of light.

Unfortunately, we do not always have the clarity of seeing in our lives how a negative experience leads to an even greater positive result. And so we can only say the blessing on negative events that, "God is a True Judge." Today we don't understand how this can be good at all; it is simply painful. Yet we believe that since the Benevolent One is a True Judge, somehow, someway, this is going to turn out good. We may not know or feel this immediately, but we can learn to trust that in the future, when all things are rectified and clear, there will only be one blessing: "God bestows good."

Divine Providence Is Always for Good Even Though We Have Free-will

Okay, maybe we can understand the *possibility* that what seems evil may be for the best. We've all heard the true stories of people who missed their flights and were very distraught. They were overwhelmed by the change in their plans and may even have been screaming at the ticket counter to be compensated, when they witness the flight they were supposed to be on crash during takeoff. We've heard many stories of people who were "prevented" from being somewhere they thought was vital, only to discover that they were saved from disaster. With this knowledge, it is easier for us to understand that in the Omnipotent One's grand plan everything can indeed be for the good.

Yet there is a very fundamental philosophical problem with this. Let's say tomorrow we have a very important business meeting at 9:00 am. We go to bed very late that night and when the alarm goes off at 7:30 am, we swat the snooze button. At 7:40 we repeat the snooze trick and by 8:00 am we have chucked our alarm on the hard floor and broken it to pieces.

When we finally wake up at 9:15 am and leap out of bed in a panic, we are in great distress! We have blown the meeting and endangered the success of our business! In the midst of our despair we suddenly remember what was discussed in this chapter and immediately comforted, we exclaim, "No problem, *gam zu le tova*, this is also for the good!"

Now does that make any sense?

We were the ones who screwed up. We are the ones who created a problem by going to bed too late at night and getting up too late in the morning. How in the world can we exonerate ourselves from responsibility by saying it's all for the good?

In other words, there is a philosophical quandary. How do we say that everything is for the good when people have free-will and can choose to do things that are bad?

Let's try to unravel this enigma. Have you ever played chess against the computer? It is a great challenge to beat the computer because the computer is able to compute all the different permutations in response and anticipation of your move. Now although it is difficult to win, it is still possible because the human being can also compute the various possible moves in response to the computer moves.

Imagine a computer that could compute an infinite number of permutations. Such a computer would be impossible to beat. The Omnipotent One has endless possibilities of how to respond and direct our actions so that whatever move we choose to make, God can still get us to where He wants us to be; to *gam zu le tova* - to this is also for the good (2*).

Let's understand this idea further. Let's say we need to reach a certain destination which would be a wonderful oasis for us. Unfortunately, we are enticed to go down a wrong path that is off to the east. Journeying down this stray road, we run into thieves and criminals who rob and harm us. Realizing this path is negative, we realign ourselves. Sadly, we still don't move towards the right locale but travel in the opposite direction of our previous detour. We are now moving west of our goal. Now we are experiencing rough terrain and getting wounded in pitfalls and ditches. At each detour we realize we are on the wrong road because of the deleterious consequences. The negative experiences in fact force us to recalculate our direction and may push us to the right path. The amazing concept is that even if we don't calibrate ourselves onto the right road, the Infinite One has endless ways to "curve" the paths to point us in the right direction and eventually get us to our real destination.

Negative Consequences Can Direct Us Towards the Good

Let's flesh out this analogy together. There is a unique mission for every individual and this is called, "One's portion in the Garden of Eden." This is our destination. If we take a circuitous route, there are limitless responses that the Omnipotent Source can provide to get us on track. One way is to show us that we have reached a wrong turn. This comes in the form of signals or negative consequences that hopefully we will learn from. Sometimes things in our lives seem to go awry and it feels like we are on the completely wrong road. The Jewish response is to reevaluate our actions and reconsider our direction. Are we doing negative things? Are we living life as we should? Are we on a dead end road?

Unfortunately, sometimes we don't change our path and maybe we "run into the thief" or "fall into the ditch" which makes us reassess our situation. This is one way in which the Omnipotent One creates a landscape, with some hills, and curves, wrong exits and mishaps which direct us towards our goal. His infinite possibilities are the methods God uses to "curve the way" to help us get where we need to go.

In our *weltanschauung* we recoil from pain and suffering. We prefer a world where there is **no** pain or suffering. We think this would be better, but would that really be the best reality? We are trying to understand that a world without pain is not a utopia. It's rather the name of a disease: *Congenital analgesia,* a rare disease where a person feels no pain. Someone with this disease can suffer from serious injuries without noticing the extent of bodily damage, including bone breakage, burns, objects in their eyes, and more, because they do not feel the pain that alerts them to injury. In young children, this can result in not treating deadly infections in time because they did not complain in any way that could alert their parents that they need treatment. The ability to feel pain is a necessary precondition to save us from harm and get us on the right track, and away from something dangerous.

Possibility for Positive Results Exists Even beyond This Reality

"Wait a minute," you protest. "This idea of sensitizing us can only apply while we are alive; if someone dies in the midst of this process, what good can it do them?" Here we need to expand our horizon. We have already seen that evil - *ra* - is seeing only a fragment of the whole picture. Therefore, if we expand our view, many things that seem evil to us can be understood in a very different way. If we could envision that the reality that we live in is not the full reality, our perspective would widen dramatically and we could overcome our tunnel vision. Thankfully we have a paradigm in our own world that can help us.

Imagine a pretend dialogue between two fetuses in the mother's womb. Let's further imagine that one of these fetuses is a so-called "realist." He only believes what he sees with his own eyes. The other fetus is the "dreamer idealist." In this story that means he believes beyond what his physical eyes can see. The dreamer tells his brother, "Someday we will be in a bigger, greater world; a world where we will see off to distant places, where we will walk on our feet and eat through our mouths." The realist scorns his dreamer brother and says, "My naïve brother, this is all there is. You got to just chill out and float around in the amniotic sac, relax and groove in the amniotic fluid." No, the dreamer protests, "I'm telling you, there is so much more to this world, another whole dimension where we will see distant sights and hear musical tones, where we will touch things and smell the fragrance of a brave new world."

"Oh you foolish dreamer," the realist sighs, "when will you face the facts, this is all there is. You should party and enjoy it now."

This argument continues for nine months. After nine months the twins experience a terrible earthquake. Their whole world shakes uncontrollably until the naïve dreamer falls away and is lost. The realist laments over his missing brother, "Oh that poor foolish dreamer, he is now gone, fallen into the abyss and lost forever." Meantime on the other side, everyone is saying, "*Mazel tov*, a baby is born!" That tumult brought a baby into a bigger and better world.

This is analogous to our reality. We can't imagine that anything exists past this dimension because this is all we see. But once we broaden our outlook and envision a reality beyond death, we can more easily understand these concepts. We can move forward to the possibilities that everything is for the good. The playing field is so much greater and so too, *gam zu le tova* is tremendously expanded.

Bringing This Concept of *Gam Zu Le Tova* into Our Emotional Realm

If we inculcate this idea *gam zu le tova*, this too is for good, into our minds and hearts, we will certainly feel empowered. This concept allows us to rely (lean = *lesmoch)* on an Entity that is not only capable of protecting us in every way but also whose purpose in creating this whole existence is to protect and bring us to that ultimate good. If we actually absorbed the meaning of this we would always feel positive, protected and happy. And to be happy is *lesmoch* - כִּשְׂמוֹחַ.

This sense of security is a foundation stone in our interaction with the outside world and is often formed by our relationship with our parents from a young age. A helpless infant must totally rely on his caretakers. When children feel that they can rely on their parents, this produces a secure vision of themselves and the world around them. This ideal relationship is hopefully then transferred to their feelings towards God Who is the ultimate Parent. And if this transference happens successfully the child will grow up into a very secure and empowered adult that can face the worst situations with the appropriate confidence.

With this perspective in mind we can solve a very strange enigma in Judaism. We all know that the Jews were given Ten Commandments on Mount Sinai which represent ten fundamental principles that are the basis of all the other commandments. When we look at the Ten Commandments more closely we see that the five commandments on the first tablet are all commandments that deal with our relationship with God: belief in God, having no other gods, etc. When we look at the second tablet we see that the five commandments there deal with directives between man and his fellow man: don't kill, don't commit adultery, don't steal, etc. There is only one apparent exception to this rule. The fifth commandment to honor our parents is on the tablet which contains the commandments between man and God. Why in the world would it be on the wrong side? We now understand it's not on the wrong side at all. The relationship between parent and child is a building block and a reflection of the relationship with God.

This doesn't mean that someone with a bad relationship with their parents will have a bad relationship with God but we often do see parallels in the two relationships. If someone grew up in a very authoritarian home they may relate to God only in the fear mode and if one's parents were very permissive, they may find it hard to imagine that God would require or demand anything from them. This parallelism is even more pronounced regarding the primal emotion of *security*. A person who deep in their psyche could never trust their parents will often transfer that feeling to God and everyone else around them. **Similarly, the healing of such a wound can also be based on redefining our relationship with the Omnipotent Source.** This is especially true in a case when the parents are not willing or able participants. When a person practices *leaning* on God and seeing the world with the eyes of *gam zu le tova*, this too is for the good, they can relearn these primal patterns.

When I was living in Israel, we lived as most Israelis do in a walk up apartment. One of my little boys had a game that he used to love to play with me as we walked up the stairs to our home. He would walk in front of me and then suddenly fall backwards and call out, "Daddy, catch me!" I would always quickly run and catch him. And I would say to him, "What are you doing? How do you know that I will catch you?" He would look up at me with a smile of confidence and say, "I know you will catch me, Daddy."

When we realize that this is the way the Almighty relates to us and that if we don't see it clearly it is only because we have partial vision (*ra*, evil), then we can feel totally empowered and allow ourselves to lean (*lesmoch*) and become truly happy (*lesmoch*).

Application One:

Identify a situation or event in your life that was difficult and painful at the time that it occurred, but now you can see it actually was for your good. Maybe it was a broken relationship which led to meeting someone better, getting fired from a job which paved the way for better employment, or maybe just a difficult time that caused you to develop in ways that you would never have done otherwise.

Meditate on this occurrence and think how you would never want or ask for such a challenge, yet another part of you realizes that without that difficulty *you would not be you*. Let yourself feel expansive and broaden your horizons as you experience your life in a larger scheme. Inculcate into your consciousness the principle that in a grander picture negative things can be for good. Know this idea and ponder it through your own personal experience with this phenomenon. Now repeat to yourself the axiom, *gam zu le tova*, this too is for the good, or a similar phrase that resonates with you.

After you have pondered this concept and connected with it on an emotional level, take an event in your life that is presently difficult. Do not start with the hardest situation. Start small and work your way up. Repeat your phrase to yourself while thinking about the situation. Let your mind wander, while the mantra of *gam zu le tova* (or anything similar) permeates your consciousness.

Now try to imagine some positive benefit this difficulty may provide you in the long run. For example, if you just lost money for a foolish thing you did, imagine that you may now make a lot more money in the future because you will be sensitive not to make this mistake again. Or maybe this money would have made you haughty and caused you greater grief. Whatever possibility you can create in your mind that is even remotely possible is sufficient. The reason why a remote possibility is enough is because by definition you can't know the correct reason! If you did, there would be no challenges or growth opportunities left for you in life. All that is therefore necessary here is to open up our narrow "tunnel vision." Knowing that there are other possibilities can help us accomplish this.

Now allow yourself to realize that somehow, in someway, in the larger scheme everything is for our ultimate good. Keep the motto of *gam zu le tova* in your head and use it whenever you can. Start applying this to small nuisances in your life, reflecting back to your own personal *gam zu le tova*, this is also for the good situation whenever necessary. Meditate on this concept and practice bringing this view into your life until you are more peaceful and confident that you are being directed in a way that is best for you.

Endnotes

(1*) The explanation in our text of how the Roman's deciphered the value of the earth is according to the philosophy/mystical approach of the Maharal, even though it differs from the simple reading of the Talmud.

(2*) In strictly philosophical terms this analogy isn't 100% accurate because God's knowledge is not like our knowledge, it doesn't change or alter based on new information or considerations. As Maimonides writes, "He is the Knower, the knowledge and the knowing; He and His knowledge are one." This concept is actually incomprehensible for mortal man and so I have presented it in the text in terms that are fathomable to us.

*Maimonides deals with this problem in explaining miracles by citing a Midrash that says all miracles were woven into the fabric of creation and were put into motion before the time they actually happened. This circumvents the problem that is implied by saying that God causes a miracle as a **response** to a particular event or series of events. In fact, it makes the computer analogy even deeper; every possible option is already built into the system even though we have free-will to act as we choose.*

CHAPTER SIX

SUFFERING AND DIVINE PROVIDENCE

....

For many of us, gam zu le tova – this too is for the good – isn't intellectually satisfying enough. We can understand the idea that we are only seeing part of the picture but still we want to know how an event that we specifically experience as bad can be good. How exactly does God "curve the paths?" This difficulty has vexed humanity from time immemorial. If you are asking this question, then you are in good company because one of the greatest in our history, our teacher Moshe asked the Endless One this very same query. Moshe asked the Almighty to reveal "His ways" and teach him, "Why do the righteous suffer and the evil prosper?"

The Talmud tells us God's answer but before we examine the response, we must face a glaring difficulty. Throughout the Tanach (Bible), the most righteous and learned prophets like Yirmiyahu scream this very same question at God. Now if God revealed the secret to Moshe, as recorded in the Talmud, why are the prophets posing the same enquiry? They can refer to the answer given to Moshe just as we can.

There are two different approaches to understand this; each one reveals another depth. The first solution is that Yirmiyahu and the other greats of history intellectually knew the answer that was given to Moshe; they are not asking for intellectual rationales at all. Instead, these great people are crying out emotionally from their pain. When someone is hurting, they scream out; it is irrelevant that this weeping will not improve things. Crying is a normal emotional response of a suffering person. This concurs with our earlier approach that we know certain things on an intellectual level but that does not preclude our need and right to experience it emotionally.

There is one crucial corollary to this idea.

When I lecture on the topic of suffering, someone will usually call out from the audience, "But how can you explain the Holocaust?" My response is, "Let's talk about the Roman Siege of Jerusalem instead, where over a million people were killed, or the massacre in the time of Bar Kochva, where nearly 600,000 people were killed, or any other historical tragedy that happened many years ago."

Why would I be willing to discuss these atrocities and not the Holocaust? The reason is because the Holocaust is too fresh in our hearts. There is no intellectual explanation that can soothe an open wound. So even if we know intellectually the answer that God told Moshe, we still cry out when we see suffering because on an emotional level, the intellectual reasoning does not assuage the pain.

The second reason why even prophets like Yirmiyahu repeated this question is not because they didn't have an answer. **Rather, it is because they had too many answers!** Moshe was told many different possibilities to explain this perplexing problem. However, regarding any individual case, you can never know which reason or combination of reasons is the precise cause. Therefore, the prophets and Sages were asking God, "Among the myriad of possible explanations, why **specifically** is this negative thing happening now?"

Rabbi Dr. Dovid Gottlieb gives the following analogy. Ask a physicist why, when a leaf falls from a tree, it lands exactly where it does. He can produce a complete list of relevant factors that affect this: the force of gravity, the motion of the air, the mass and aerodynamic properties of the leaf, etc., which all determine the leaf's downward path.

Now suppose there is a leaf still attached to the tree, and we ask the physicist to mark the exact spot on the ground where it will land when it falls ten seconds from now. He cannot do it. Does this show that his explanation of why the leaf falls the way it does, is wrong? Not at all. He has cited all the relevant factors, but he cannot quantify them in a particular case. He cannot ascertain the exact motion of all the molecules of air in the vicinity, the exact aerodynamic characteristics of the leaf and so on. His explanation applies to leaves generally, but cannot be applied in detail to any specific leaf. Similarly, the Jewish explanations of suffering will apply generally, but will not be able to explain in detail particular cases of suffering.

So let us begin with some of the possible causes for suffering. Each individual reason will not suffice to explain why the righteous suffer or the evil prosper, but if we consider the entire gamut of reasons, we may get some sense of how the Omnipotent One "curves the paths" to bring everything to good.

We will begin with approaches that are connected to our own actions. These levels were revealed to Moshe. Later we will see other rationales for suffering that surpass our limited human perspective. Concerning these rationales God told Moshe, "A man cannot see Me and live."

Now in the category of sufferings connected with our actions, we will focus on two types: what I call the "educational approach" and the "rectifying consequences approach." Let's begin with the "educational approach."

The Educational Approach

As we discussed earlier, if there was no pain sensation in this world it would not create a paradise but rather a rare disease called *congenital analgesia*. Pain allows us to learn from our surroundings and alter or adapt our behaviors to make them positive and productive. If we are exercising in a way that causes us pain and damages our bodies, it may indicate that we are using our muscles in a deleterious manner and need to change our form. Similarly, when we do things that are spiritually harmful we may receive a response that is painful. **This painful response may be like a spiritual warning siren.** It is supposed to alert us to adjust our direction because we are traveling along a negative path. If we are transforming into a "business shark" or an unfaithful spouse and we run into some trouble, we shouldn't be so fast to push our problems aside. The barriers we encounter may actually be road blocks to inspire us to reconsider our way. These sufferings are called educational because their purpose is to educate us to live correctly.

If these educational sufferings do not cause us to change our path immediately, that doesn't mean that they haven't been successful. Sometimes we may actually learn the lesson through experiencing the difficulties themselves. The Talmud records an unbelievable story of the sufferings of a righteous man and how he became even greater by going through these difficulties. However, before we retell this story I need to convey a certain spiritual rule. The rule is that the expectations for great people are very grand and they are evaluated according to a higher standard. This allows them to achieve even more greatness, as discussed earlier, but these standards for the average person could be nonsensical. So don't freak out when you hear this story; realize that the protagonist was a very great man and he was functioning on his own level. The lesson we can learn is that suffering may lead to positive change and that idea applies to everyone.

The Jewish leader at the end of the second century of the Common Era, was the illustrious Rabbi Yehudah HaNasi (the Prince), who was affectionately known as Rebbe (our Rabbi). One day he was walking down the road and a butcher was leading a calf to the slaughter. The calf ran away from the butcher and placed its head under Rebbe's cloak as if he was hiding from the butcher. Rebbe ordered the calf to go back to the butcher and exclaimed, "Go! For this you were created." Rebbe's apparent lack of sensitivity for the calf elicited a response from Above that caused Rebbe to experience tremendous physical agony for thirteen years. His suffering was very great. After thirteen years of this incredible pain you can be sure that Rebbe had changed and became an even more sensitive and spiritual luminary than before.

One day he was in his house and his maid found some weasels. She was about to sweep them up and dispose of them, when Rebbe called out, "Leave them alone." As the verse says, "God is compassionate on all His creatures." At that moment the tremendous sufferings left him.

This is an example of sufferings to educate us, where the sufferings themselves become our mentor. Many of us have had harrowing experiences in our lives that ended up being the impetus for true change and growth, whether it is the famous story of the surfer girl who lost her arm and reassessed her values or a person who experienced hatred and through that ordeal developed tremendous sensitivity to help and educate others. These types of lessons are the stuff that historical figures are made of. If we look deeply into our own lives, we can certainly find difficulties that caused us to rethink our values and challenges that made us who we are today. This is the educational approach.

The Rectifying Consequences Approach

The next approach is what I call "rectifying consequences." It also presumes a connection between our actions and the difficulties we sometimes experience in life; therefore, we must digress to explain the underpinnings of this idea. The whole concept that our actions can be a cause of our troubles disturbs modern man to no end. People become belligerent when you introduce this approach. "Are you saying I am being punished?" they incredulously ask. Their irritation is in some ways justifiable and in some ways it is not. We must therefore delve into the basis of this rationale and understand our visceral reaction to it.

So let's go.

If someone tells you that you are suffering for a particular reason, your desire to punch them in the nose may not be so wrong. Unless the person edifying you is a prophet or an enlightened Sage, there is no way they can know that a specific suffering is due to a specific action. Consequently, it would be audacious for anyone to explain why any individual suffers. On the other hand, to make that assumption for *ourselves* is certainly a commendable way to approach life. The Talmud even tells us, "if someone sees suffering come upon them, they should assess their actions and see if they are acting erroneously." This doesn't mean that you will know for sure why something negative is happening to you **but if your assumption leads to positive change then you are on the right path.**

Often we can't imagine our actions as the source of our difficulties because we feel we aren't *so bad* to deserve such negativity. I certainly understand that emotion but here are a few points to consider that may broaden our perspective.

Imagine you were doing a project that would earn you ten billion dollars. Since the reward is so great, wouldn't you assume there would be high expectations? Furthermore, if you were specifically chosen for this multi-billion-dollar venture, wouldn't that indicate that your potential is much higher than you previously thought? In this world the stakes are high and we often don't realize our latent greatness. Yes, it is hard to correlate our suffering to our deficiencies but that is because we don't fully appreciate the worth of our actions. When you consider that the stakes in life are so high, the rewards are so great, and that you can attain so much, you begin to see beyond your own difficulties. Therefore, the Talmud advises someone who is suffering to first investigate their deeds. Maybe they are doing something wrong. However, if you check and see that you aren't acting negatively, the next step is **to examine if you are maximizing your potential** because your potential is probably a lot greater than you ever imagined. (1*)

Consequences for Actions

Unfortunately, there is one more reason that we may refuse to look into our own actions as a potential source of suffering and this reason is flawed. It is our scorn towards the dreaded idea of reward and punishment. We recoil from this whole concept as some remnant from a repressive Victorian worldview of a vengeful god that destroyed evil doers. Civilization has advanced and freed itself from these medieval fears of Divine retribution that dominated a superstitious society. Yet if we analyze the premise of reward and punishment we will see the rational for **its existence and necessity.**

Imagine that you and an acquaintance are both employed for the same company. You are a dedicated worker putting in seventy hours of work each week while your acquaintance spends most of his time on coffee break and puts in the equivalent of five unfocused hours of work each week. At the end of the month you both receive your pay checks and your pay is exactly the same as his. You go to your boss and complain that this is completely unfair! Your boss consoles you and tells you not to take it so hard, saying, "It's just that at this company we don't like to work with the old fashioned reward and punishment system."

Would you ever accept such a response? Not a chance.

Everyone knows that reward and punishment is the only fair way. So maybe what bothers us is the misguided impression of the Omnipotent One as a vengeful god. You remember when you were young and your parents got angry with you, and their punishment was not always meted out in a loving way that could redirect you. Sometimes they just flew off the handle and their punishment was more to assuage their anger than to teach you. In the case of the Omnipotent One nothing can be further from the truth. **Every punishment is in order to redirect and purify us; and every punishment is directly connected to the negative act and a potential solution for it.**

So let's change the terminology and call this process "actions and consequences." Pretend that I recommended a new diet for you called the Amazing Ingber Diet. It consists of a half-gallon of ice cream and eight large cookies for breakfast, cotton candy and coke for lunch, and for dinner, all of the above plus a bag of Snickers bars. After a week of this indulgence you come to me holding your stomach and complaining about how awful you feel. You then ask me why I punished you. I explain that I didn't punish you at all; this is simply the consequence for listening to such an idiotic diet. In fact, your nauseous feeling and inability to hold down anything except for some foul-tasting medicine **is part of your healing process**.

Let's now try to understand the mystical root of "action and consequence" and then we can appreciate how sufferings can be rectifying consequences.

In the Image of God (E-lo-him), Being Empowered to Affect the System

The Torah tells us that humanity was created in the image of God. However, if we are exacting in the language of the text, there is a very specific Name of God used in this context; it says we are made *betzelem Elokim*, in the "image of *Elokim*." Why is this Name Elokim used and not the Tetragrammaton? The Tetragrammaton is the essential four letter Name of God that consists of the conjugation of the verb "is" in the past, present and future tenses, representing that God "was, is and always will be." He is beyond any concept of time and space and makes everything else *be*.

The obvious answer why we are not made in the image of that Name is because we don't resemble God in that aspect at all; we are not limitless and unfathomable. "Okay, I can understand that," we say, "but if so, what does it mean to be in the image of *Elokim*?" What relationship do we have with the Name *Elokim* and what can it possibly mean to be in God's image anyway when He has **no image**?

Let's try to unravel this difficult concept. For starters we must realize that we cannot understand God's essence in any way. As the Holy Zohar says, לית מחשבה תפיסיה ביה כלל "*Layes machshavah tefisah b'yah klal*"-no mind can fathom Him at all. Therefore, all the various Names of God refer to different ways that He is manifested to us. He chooses to relate to us in different ways at different times. Sometimes He manifests the aspect of justice, other times compassion, or kindness. **The various Names**

of God correlate to those different manifestations. The most we can comprehend is how the Endless One *chooses to relate to us*. Regarding His Essence, we have no concept and no Name to refer to at all.

The Name *Elokim* connotes the Master of all powers. When God refers to Himself as *Elokim*, He is revealing how He directs every aspect of creation and completely controls every detail. "Wait a moment," you may say, "aren't those the details of the system we call nature and when God *gets involved* it's what we call a miracle?" No, that is a misconception. So first we must understand how *Elokim* is the Master of all powers, both the miraculous (2*) and natural. Then we'll appreciate the significance of being created in that image.

God in Miracles and Nature

So let's ponder an event that would be considered a miracle by all: the story of the splitting of the Red Sea. In the Biblical account, the Egyptians have the Jews trapped by the Red Sea, when suddenly the sea parts, allowing the Jews to escape. The open pathway lures the pursuing Egyptians into the sea but the waters then collapse upon them and they drown. This is obviously an incredible open miracle.

Now let's do a mind experiment. Pretend that the Red Sea split at a specific time every seventy years. Would you call that event a miracle? Certainly not. We have a name for that type of an occurrence. It is called a phenomenon. As a matter of fact, if the Red Sea split every seventy years, people would gather by the sea on their lawn chairs, CNN would televise the event and it would make for good educational TV. No miracle.

Now let's imagine further that the Red Sea split every single day. Would that be a miracle? Of course not. We would just call that "nature." We would search for a scientific explanation to understand what happens in the natural world to invoke the parting of water. Is it the tides? Maybe it's magnetic fields?

Our Sages contend that when the Red Sea split, all waters in the world separated, so maybe the scientific explanation would be on the atomic level? Either way, we would do what science does so well, explain *how* the process works. We would not ask the philosophical question of *why* the system should be that way at all. Such a question is not in the purview of science. But with all our scientific marvel at the beauty of nature, the splitting of the Red Sea would become a nature experience to us, just like trees growing and caterpillars' morphing into butterflies.

Imagine all waters split every day at exactly 12 pm noon. In no time at all the experience would be completely common place. You would be at the pool with your family and the life guard would blow his whistle at 11:55 am and announce, "Okay, everyone out of the pool, waters are about to split!" You wouldn't bat an eye about this announcement; this is such a common occurrence!

However, if we ask ourselves what is really the difference between the sea splitting every day, or every seventy years, or just once in history, the actual difference is only **frequency.** The act has not changed, just how often it is experienced. And so the mystics define a miracle as the will of the Creator one time in history, while nature is His "ongoing will." The *Kabbalists* cite a passage that reads, "He renews in every day, in every moment, the act of creation." This fantastic insight teaches us that the world was not formed and then continues functioning on automatic pilot. Rather, existence is consistently being recreated and reality is constantly being reformed. What a mind-boggling transformative way to see the world and thereby our ability to renew ourselves!

Yet it is the Creator's will that the existence that comes into being at every moment is the same existence as the moment before. That is His "ongoing will" and we experience this as "nature." Therefore, we see in *gematria,* the mystical numerological system where every letter has a numerical value, i.e., Aleph = 1, Bet = 2, etc., that the Name *Elokim* is exactly the same as the Hebrew word for nature, *Hateva*, both being 86. This is because *Elokim* is the Source of everything that we call the "natural processes." In fact, the word *Hateva*, nature, is rooted in the word *Tevoa*, which means to drown, because if a person isn't careful he can *drown in nature* and believe it has some power of its own and is not rooted in an ultimate Source. As we see, people often attribute the wonders of the world to "Mother Nature."

My mother's name is not "Nature" and I'm sure yours isn't either but this colloquialism is part of the problem. The attempt to disconnect nature from its Source is a very dangerous process. It is a process that can drown us and make us ignore the cause of the daily natural miracles that surround us. Alternatively, the word for nature, *teva*, can also mean a signet or stamp - *tevat*. Nature is not an independent entity. Rather, it is the expression of God's will. It is His stamp, His signet and He is the Source of it all. The Name of God which signifies this concept is the Name *Elokim*. Consequently, if we rearrange the letters of the Name *Elokim* it spells, *Me Elo* (מי אלה = א-כ'ל'הים), which literally means, "who… these." When we see the ongoing wonders that we call "nature," we need to ask ourselves, "**Who** made and controls all **these** things?" The answer is *Elokim*. "Nature" is the "ongoing will" of the Creator that challenges us to see through it and not drown in it! If you see Godliness in a beautiful sunset, a smile on a loved one's face or a chance meeting with someone that enhances your life, then you are seeing the Divine in everything and living a spiritual life.

In the Image of Elokim Means We Directly Affect the Universe

Now when God created humanity, in a certain sense, *He gave us the keys to the creation*. Our positive actions directly cause the world to flourish while our negative actions actually damage the universe. Amazingly, in that sense we are truly made in the image of *Elokim*!

Let's explore the tremendous depth in this concept. We know that there are laws of the physical world. We realize that we can't float up into the sky because of gravity. Objects fall *down*, not *up*. We see that for every action there is an equal and opposite reaction. Yet when it comes to spiritual matters we think that it's a free for all. This is certainly not the case. ***The spiritual laws are not only as binding as the physical laws but they are actually the roots of the physical laws.*** Just as there are wavelengths beyond our visual range and sound waves that we cannot hear, there are entire spiritual universes that are outside our sensory perception. These spiritual worlds parallel our physical world and every aspect of the physical dimension has a corresponding spiritual force that is the root cause of everything that occurs here. A blade of grass on earth doesn't grow until the spiritual force in charge of the grass strikes it to grow. The general structural model of the world is that when the Omnipotent One directs things to happen in this world the action is initiated in the spiritual realms and it then flows down to the physical dimension.

Since God wanted humankind to complete themselves and the entire universe too, humans were created as a conglomeration of the entire world. Everything that exists in the physical world is somehow contained in our nature. And since the physical dimension parallels the spiritual realms, we also parallel the spiritual worlds. So although I can't explain to you what your body looks like in a spiritual dimension, I can tell you that the form, structure and meaning of your being in this world is exactly reflected in a non-physical higher dimension. Each spiritual dimension becomes more refined than the spiritual world below it.

Our Sages teach us that our bodies are constructed of 248 essential limbs and 365 essential sinews (including muscular systems that hold the body together). Furthermore, our bodies are the parallel to our souls. As the mystics say, at its root, the body and soul are one unified entity, the soul arising from the *refined light* and the body coming from the *coarser aspect of that light.* Although it is absurd to speak about the soul in terms of parts, yet the soul parallels the body's system of 248 limbs and 365 sinews in a spiritual sense.

This is obviously not arbitrary. If you count the amount of *mitzvot*, you will find there are 248 positive commandments and 365 negative commandments. Every commandment corresponds to a part of the body as well as to an aspect of the soul. Consequently, fulfilling the *mitzvot* leads to physical and spiritual health.

Moreover, since we now know that man is a microcosm of all the worlds, we can know that **there is a direct link between our actions and the state of the universe.** If one does a positive act with one's right arm (the *mitzvah* which correlates to one's right arm in body and soul), one will (so to speak) strengthen the right arm of the spiritual worlds that one parallels. This will cause a chain reaction going up to the highest spiritual realm which will then rebound back through the spiritual worlds reaching the physical universe and causing a positive reaction in this physical world.

The ramifications of this concept are astonishing. Perfecting the world (what is often called *Tikkun Olam*) isn't necessarily about social activism but rather it is woven into the fabric of all creation. When you are sitting alone in the privacy of your own home and you do a positive act, **you are building the spiritual worlds and actually causing this physical dimension to become a better place too.** Similarly, the belief that we can do whatever we want to ourselves is now exposed as erroneous. We are all in the boat together and if someone drills a hole beneath their cabin they affect the entire ship. More precisely, every time you do an action with your body, say a word with your mouth or entertain a thought in your mind, you are either strengthening or damaging the spiritual world that correlates to that part of you as well as the physical world we all live in.

Now after this long and complex introduction we can finally understand how reward and punishment are really **action and consequence.** Since God gave us the means to perfect ourselves and the world, our actions have tremendous ramifications. We are made in the image of *Elokim*, the Master of all powers. When you give someone complete access to a nuclear power plant, they can harness energy to build or destroy. And so with us, every one of our actions causes incredible reverberations for each of us personally and for the entire system. So let's not call it reward and punishment but rather let's understand that since our beings are linked up to the structure of the universe there are direct *consequences* for everything we do.

There is one caveat to the paradigm of action and consequence that we must recognize. Although our actions are integrally aligned with the entire structure, there is a limit to what we can do. We cannot destroy or derail the system. So even though our actions cause far reaching effects, the Omnipotent One still directs every aspect of existence and His Providence brings the world to its ultimate goal. This Providence is amazingly blended with our free-will in a symphony that is way beyond our grasp. So although the consequences of our actions are always expressed, it can be conveyed in a myriad of possible processes. For example, if someone commits a negative action and a negative response is due to them, the Omnipotent One may delay the response so that the individual will have time to correct the deed by doing *teshuvah*, allowing them to undo the negative repercussion. Alternatively, maybe the perpetrator is destined to father a very righteous child in the future, so the negative consequences are postponed until after the child is born. The type of response, the timing of the response, the affect it has on everyone involved, are just some of the many factors that the Omnipotent One blends and weaves together to bring the world to its completion in the face of our free-will.

Okay, you say, I understand we are created in a way to affect the entire universe. I also recognize that our actions will thereby cause tremendous consequences, but what does this have to do with the second reason of suffering, rectifying consequences?

Let me explain.

Experiencing the Consequences in a Temporal or Eternal Realm

Imagine that you have lived your life righteously. Let's pretend you can put a number on it and you can say that you've done one hundred good acts that will produce one hundred positive consequences. And you have done only three negative acts that produce three negative responses. Now you are given a choice: would you prefer to get all one hundred positive consequences as well as the three negative consequences or would you rather just have the three negatives cancel three positives and get ninety-seven positive consequences? Most people instinctively say they want the ninety-seven positives.

We hate pain; but we really shouldn't be so hasty. First we need to appreciate the magnitude of the reward we will receive before we are willing to give it up.

To see this principle in action we will spotlight one of the supreme degenerates of all time. There was a man who killed and maimed without restraint and in fact was only credited with doing three good things in his life. The man's name was Nebuchadnezzar. He eventually became the king of Babylon. The Talmud asks what positive acts this malefactor did in order to merit becoming the king. Here's the story.

As a young man, Nebuchadnezzar was the scribe to the king of Babylon. At that time, the Babylonian king wanted to send a message to the king of Judea whose name was Hezekiah (in Hebrew, Chizkiyahu). The king dictated the letter to Nebuchadnezzar with the preface "Peace be upon thee, King Chizkiyahu. Peace be upon thee, city of Jerusalem and peace be upon thee, God of the Jews." Nebuchadnezzar wrote the dictation but thought to himself that the letter was improperly addressed. It should have been written, "Peace be upon thee, God of the Jews, peace be upon thee, city of Jerusalem and peace be upon thee, King Chizkiyahu." He felt that God certainly deserves more honor than Jerusalem or the king of Judea. Nebuchadnezzar then ran three strides to retrieve the king and have him readdress the letter. Incredibly, those three steps that Nebuchadnezzar took earned him the right to rule over the world for three generations!

So we see that the reward for positive actions is very great. We should not be so fast to cancel out any of the ramifications of our good deeds.

However, this story is extremely bizarre. All in all, Nebuchadnezzar was a terrible person; why should he be rewarded? And besides that, we have all done good things in our lives and none of us has gotten to rule the world!

The Omnipotent One is righteous and just in every way and therefore no deed can be ignored. Every action causes a response, whether it is a righteous person committing an evil act or an evil person doing a righteous act. Since the world was created so that we can earn our way, nothing is omitted. Nebuchadnezzar's positive act created a positive response. The question is just what type of recompense should he receive? You see, there are two completely different types of payment: one is physical and the other is spiritual, **though sometimes compensation is in both and sometimes they are even completely interconnected**. Spiritual reward and consequence is eternal but physical reward and consequence is temporal. So where would we prefer to get paid? Do we want our reward in the physical dimension, with say eighty years of fun? Or would we prefer payment that is eternal?

Generally speaking, the scales are tilted in our favor and when payment can only be in this reality or the next, we get paid in the greater currency: eternity. Nebuchadnezzar, though, represents a different type of person, a person who is so thoroughly evil that he has no interest in spiritual currency. Such a person can receive all their positive consequences in this temporal reality **as they prefer,** so that there is nothing positive left for the world to come. But remember, the reward is still very great, just like it would need to be in eternal currency. Nebuchadnezzar's small acts were paid in full in this reality and so his reward and consequence in this world was total domination.

Now imagine how great our payments will be in the eternal currency. It is therefore nonsensical to cancel out any of our positive deeds. **The best deal we can hope for is to get paid back the three negative consequences in this temporal reality and get the full payment for the one hundred good deeds in eternal currency.**

This is what we call "rectifying consequences." Even righteous people do negative things in life and there are consequences to their negative actions. If they do not reverse the deed by doing *teshuvah*, repentance, **the consequence is the medicine that rectifies what they have done.** The best place to pay off that "debt" is in this reality, not the next; *that is why sometimes righteous people suffer in this life.*

Furthermore, imagine someone gives you a million-dollar loan with no repayment conditions. Although you realize you have a debt, for now you are extremely happy. Let's now picture that one day your creditor shows up at your door unannounced and demands payment in full. Your elation vanishes into thin air and you wish that you would have set up a payment plan. In truth, the greatest kindness would have been minuscule payments over an incredibly long period of time.

That is exactly what God does for us. Sometimes when we have created negative consequences the Benevolent One gives us tiny doses of the consequence that we can handle. Even the slightest misfortune like ordering hot soup but getting cold soup instead is considered partial payment for our negativity. So when small hassles happen to us, instead of getting frustrated, think that we may be paying off a negative consequence and thereby keeping our positive actions fully intact. If we can do this, we will deal with life's bumps in a totally positive, productive and happy perspective.

Let's summarize rectifying consequences.

1.   There are spiritual worlds that parallel the physical world.

2.   Actions are initiated in the spiritual realms and are transmitted to the physical realm via a step down system (from the highest to lowest level).

3.   The Omnipotent One created human beings as a microcosm of these spiritual dimensions, in the image of *Elokim* - with the power to affect the world.

4. Therefore, our actions, by definition, cause positive or negative consequences individually and collectively.

5. We experience the consequences of our actions. The experience of positive actions is joy and the experience of negative actions is distress.

6. Experiencing distress as a consequence of negative actions is one way to abrogate the negative act; it becomes part and parcel of the healing remedy.

7. A virtuous person that creates some negative consequences may experience those consequences in this reality so as not to taint their experience of the positive in a higher eternal dimension.

An Example of Rectifying Consequences

This lesson is brought out in a Talmudic narrative. One time the greatest Sage of the generation, Rabbi Eliezer, was ill. His students stood around him, crying at the sight of their beloved and holy leader suffering. Then in walked another one of Rabbi Eliezer's students, the famous Rabbi Akivah. Upon comprehending the magnitude of the situation before him, Rabbi Akivah began to laugh.

His colleagues were outraged, "Rabbi Akivah, how can you possibly laugh at such a time?" they demanded to know.

"Why are you crying?" Rabbi Akivah responded.

The other students were beside themselves, "the light of the world is suffering, how we can not cry?" they rejoined.

Rabbi Akivah told them that was exactly why he was laughing. He explained, "All my life I observed that our teacher Rabbi Eliezer was always successful. His wine never went bad and his business dealings never failed. I began to wonder to myself, is it possible that our teacher is getting paid some of his eternal reward (consequence) in this world? Now that I see him having these difficulties, I know that his eternal reward is fully intact for the world to come, since he is receiving some negative consequences in this reality for whatever mistakes he has made, even if they are small and inadvertent."

Upon hearing this, Rabbi Eliezer responded, "You have comforted me Akivah."

Let's summarize what we have learned so far:

1. There are many possible reasons why righteous people may suffer but we cannot know which particular reason or combination of reasons is at hand.

2. One possible reason is educational; challenges that can lead to change.

3. Another possible reason can be rectifying consequences where the difficulties we experience are themselves remedies for our negative actions.

These approaches connect our shortcomings with our sufferings. We can add to this group suffering brought on by a person's own recklessness. Obviously if a person takes insane risks and abuses his or her body they are to blame for their situation. In such a case we do not need to search for metaphysical reasons.

All our rationales for suffering so far in this chapter are included in the Talmudic adage we quoted earlier: One who experiences suffering should first check out their deeds. Maybe they are doing something wrong. If not, they should verify if they are maximizing their potential.

However, the Talmud continues: If you **are** maximizing your potential then your difficulties cannot be attributed to your actions, rather they are of a different type all together. These are called *Yesurim shel Ahavah* – Sufferings of Love. This category is much more difficult to comprehend.

We can grasp it only in the general sense because to fully fathom this would require knowing the essence of every individual and the entire scheme of reality, which we cannot do. It is included in God's response to Moshe, "You cannot see My face; because a man cannot see Me and live." The text says that although God did not show Moshe His face, He did show Moshe His "back." What is the meaning of such a statement, since God has neither a literal face nor a literal back?

When you see your friend's face you know clearly it is him. Indeed, the word for face in Hebrew is *panim* (פָּנִים), which also means "inside" (פְּנִים). This is because your face is a window into your essence. Moshe wanted to know how God runs His world and why sometimes the righteous suffer and the evil prosper. God's response is that you can get a general idea but not a complete picture, similar to seeing your friend from behind where you think it's him but you cannot be sure.

Additionally, the word face, *panim* (פָּנִים) comes from the word *panei* (פְּנֵה) which means "to turn toward the direction you are traveling." God told Moshe that you can't see My *panim*, i.e., you cannot understand where I am **heading beforehand**. It is only after everything is done, i.e., from the back, that you can perceive the path I took. Only after the entire symphony is complete can you comprehend why every aspect transpired in the way it did (i.e., from behind) but as the process is still unfolding it cannot be fully recognized (i.e., while still facing in that direction). The details of Sufferings of Love are one of those things that cannot be fully fathomed by mortal humans. Still, a general understanding is possible and crucial.

So let us begin. What is this Suffering of Love? How can *love* be the cause of suffering if we haven't done anything negative to deserve the suffering?

Sufferings That Are Not a Response to Our Actions

Let's try to unravel this mystery through an ancient text called the Midrash. The Midrash asks why God tests the greatest of people. The Midrash gives the following three parables.

1. When you want to make flax soft and usable in the finest way you must beat the flax; so too the righteous must sometimes get walloped.

2. In ancient times when a potter wanted to sell his wares, he banged the pots so people would hear the sound and realize how durable his clay pots were. Just as you have to bang on the strong pots which don't break, so too the righteous and strong are hit because they can take it.

3. If you needed to plow a large, rough field, would you place the yoke on the weakest ox or the strongest? Of course the plow would go on the strongest so it can accomplish the task. So too the heaviest load is given to the greatest people.

Now all these different analogies are nice but they seem very redundant. Why does the Midrash need to give me three different examples: flax, pots and an ox? Couldn't we have understood the point with just one example?

If you think carefully about the three items mentioned you'll realize that they represent different types of relationships: flaxes are beaten in order to improve *the flax themselves*, the pot is banged for *the benefit of the observer* and the ox is laden with the yoke for *the improvement of the field*. So too, the great challenges that befall a person. Sometimes they are specifically for his or her good, sometimes they assist others, and other times they improve the world on the whole.

Let's analyze each relationship.

Difficulties That Make You Greater

The flax analogy represents suffering or challenges that are not in response to negative actions, but in order to increase one's positive experience for eternity. It's possible that an extremely righteous person can go through great difficulties in life not because they did anything wrong but rather in order to become refined and developed. Just as flax becomes soft and superior by being beaten, at times we become greater through the challenges we endure. This refinement doesn't only raise one in this reality but also the hardships one undergoes in this world can actually give us a richer, fuller experience in the world to come. Often our potential greatness is only brought to the fore when we face great adversity. This is the "beating of the flax" that makes us better.

Difficulties That Help Others

Other times the difficulties that righteous people go through may be for the benefit of others, as in the analogy of the beaten pots. This concept needs a lot of explanation because Christian theology has made this idea central to its belief system and the alteration of this idea from its original Jewish sources has made the Christian concept antithetical to Jewish belief.

In Jewish thought we understand that there is an interconnection between people. This is revealed in the teaching that when the Jews crossed over the Jordan River into the Land of Israel they accepted to be guarantors for each other. On a mystical level this refers to the souls being completely intertwined and individual souls being part of a greater soul. The name Israel (Yisrael) is an acronym for *yesh shishim rebo otiyot laTorah*, which means there are six hundred thousand letters of the Torah. What is the connection between Israel and the letters of the Torah? The connection is that every Jew has a corresponding letter in the Torah and just as there are 600,000 letters in the Torah so too there are 600,000 Jews. (3*)

Now that is very bizarre. Although the number of eligible males for the army when the Jews were in the desert was essentially that number, there were more Jews in that generation, and certainly if we combine all the Jews throughout the generations, there have been more than 600,000 Jews. Rather, the 600,000 Jews that parallel 600,000 letters of the Torah **refer to the 600,000 Jewish souls**. How can there be 600,000 Jewish souls and more than 600,000 Jews?

To understand this, picture the components of the human body and you will realize that although there are distinct, separate organs, they combine together to create one organism. So too, each individual soul is part of a greater soul, just as limbs and organs combine to make one body. There are 600,000 of these soul units which are comprised of many individual souls. Additionally, these 600,000 souls combine into one grand soul called *Knesset Yisroel*, the Congregation of Israel. Consequently, a person can be compared to a different body part which represents the mission for the overall organism. This can also explain why sometimes we feel an instant bond with another person: we may be part of the same root soul or we may have a similar task to do in this life, which would mean that we are, metaphorically, the same limb!

Now due to this interconnectedness it is possible that one part of the organism can take on a heavier load for the rest of the organism. If one breaks one's right foot, one compensates for one's deficiency by putting more weight on the left foot. So too a righteous person may sometimes willingly accept difficulties for the greater good of others. Of course the righteous person will eventually receive even more reward because of this sacrifice. However, this system only works if the righteous person willingly and lovingly accepts these difficulties for the greater entity.

Please realize that this system does not exonerate the general populace from their responsibilities. They are still required to act morally and are judged accordingly. It is just that to some degree there is an amelioration of the immediate consequences due them. We can see a similar concept in our own societies where people sacrifice for others and thereby remove certain negative effects. In 1892, Dr. Max Von Pettenkofer exposed himself to cholera to save the lives of others. In 1900, Dr. Walter Reed's research team infected themselves with yellow fever as part of the research that ultimately saved countless lives. This type of suffering of the righteous is for the good of others, just like the clay pots that are beaten to show *others* how resilient they are.

Difficulties for the Universal Good

The third comparison, to the robust ox, represents an unbelievably righteous individual whose challenges and difficulties are actually part of the rectification of the entire scheme of reality. Just like the powerful ox is needed to plow the rocky field, these individual's difficulties are part of the cosmic remedy, as we explained in Chapter Two, regarding Rabbi Elazar's suffering as a unique mission that was part of the grand design. All these righteous people ultimately will be rewarded for their own deeds as well as the role they accomplished for the entire world. They will be fully compensated for their sufferings, making it well worth it to them personally, as well.

So although on one hand good people receive goodness, protection and assistance, there are many reasons why sometimes the righteous suffer. There is even a meta-rule that dictates that this must be the case. Imagine a world where righteous people only flourished and evil people were only maligned. Could free-will exist in such a world? Certainly not; it would be too obvious for all to act righteously. The seeming injustice and non-clarity it produces are necessary components to earn reward. In fact, it even allows the righteous to demonstrate that they are acting sincerely and not just for reward.

Another Rationale for "Undeserved" Suffering Are Actions in a Previous Life

There is one more possible rationale for seemingly undeserved suffering that we must discuss. This concept was concealed in ancient Jewish writings and was simply referred to as *Sod Haibor,* "the secret of gestation." This mystical concept was not relayed to the masses as it can be seriously misunderstood and thereby cause great damage. Today, the general concept has been heard by many, though understood by few; it is called *gilgulim*, or in English, reincarnation.

The Jewish concept of *gilgulim* differs significantly from other approaches to this idea. In *gilgulim* the person's soul may come back into this world in another body in order to rectify or complete a lacking from a past life. Therefore, a person can be born with various challenges or limitations based on the root of their soul and how they functioned in a previous life. For example, it was reported that an autistic child was brought before a *Kabbalistic* Sage in Israel and the Sage stood up before the boy. This seemed very unusual, as the custom is that a regular person needs to stand up in honor of a Torah Sage, to honor the Torah he has learned, not the other way around. When the Rabbi's students asked him to explain his behavior, he told them that he perceived this boy's soul and that the boy's soul was on a very high level of perfection. He stood up in honor of the boy's essence. The Sage noted that in fact this soul had nothing left to perfect in this world other than it had spoken negatively in a past *gilgul,* thus the soul came back with a communication impediment as a means of remediation.

We see that the purpose of *gilgulim* is to achieve perfection and to rectify the self and the world. It is not that the conscious is in a constant recycling until it is freed from sequences of life and death. The *gilgul* is an opportunity to continue the *tikkun* (rectifying) process. As a matter of fact, if a person after four *gilgulim* has only regressed, this mode of achieving completion is removed from them. The fact that there are *gilgulim* doesn't mean that the soul wants to come back to this realm. Just as the soul originally was basking in the Supernal Light and only reluctantly entered this world to earn its connection, so too, the soul preferably does not want to return as a *gilgul.* However, the Omnipotent One chooses from amongst His endless possible ways the ideal method to bring us to completion in order to experience the Infinite. Some methods of completion involve experiencing consequences of actions after death. Others involve our experiences during life and sometimes wholeness can be attained by returning to this life to finish the job. This is the concept of *gilgul*.

There are many deep and intricate factors in *gilgulim*. One important idea to know is that there are different levels of the soul itself. We talk about five dimensions of the soul: *Nefesh, Ruach, Neshamah, Chaya, Yechidah*. A person has to earn the ability to access all the aspects of his or her soul. When a person is born, one only receives the *Nefesh* level. When one becomes of age one can receive access to the next level, *Ruach*, and so on. Additionally, a person needs to complete all levels of the soul and consequently one may well need to come back to this world to do that. This means that the simple understanding that a *gilgul* is one soul that occupied two different bodies is not entirely accurate. Rather it can be that one body may have the *Nefesh* of a particular soul while the later *gilgul* may have the *Ruach* of the same soul, etc. Understanding this concept can clarify many questions about resurrection and soul mates.

It is also important to note that the soul is the essence of the person. As opposed to some schools of Eastern thought, there is definitely a "self" that is the person's soul. When the individual receives ultimate reward in the World to Come and connects fully to the Divine, the individual is still there as an entity that has earned this connection. This is a fantastic and unique idea! It is analogous to the flame of a candle that becomes united with an enormous fire and yet the candle-fire still somehow remains a candle-fire. This paradox is part of the pleasure of the World to Come where we connect totally with the Divine and yet there is a sense of our unique soul consciousness.

Years ago I was told the following story. I cannot say if it is a true story or not but the principle is certainly true and so I will share it with you. The story begins with a Chassidic Rabbi in Poland. One extremely harsh freezing day, the Rabbi gathered ten of his students, a wagon driver and a *mohel* (a person trained to perform circumcision) and asked them to set out with him on a journey. The Rabbi told the wagon driver to head out of the town and that he would direct him where to go. Meanwhile, the weather worsened into a treacherous snow storm and the wagon driver couldn't see anything amidst the white blanket of flurries. The Rabbi kept encouraging the driver to continue forward until he spotted a small house in the distance. He told the wagon driver to navigate towards it.

When the Rabbi and his entourage arrived at the house, they knocked on the door. The door flung open and a man recognized the famous Rabbi, greeted him with profuse warmth and invited the assembly to enter. The owner of the house hurriedly explained that eight days ago his wife gave birth to a son and he had planned to drive into town to have the child circumcised but the weather had been so bad he was afraid to take the child outside. The Rabbi comforted the man, "well, you are very fortunate because we have a quorum for the circumcision and we even have a *mohel* with us."

"Amazing," they all exclaimed. The circumcision was performed and there was a great celebration. The Rabbi and students spent the day enjoying time with the family. Unfortunately, towards the end of the day tragedy struck and a blood curdling scream was heard from the bedroom; the baby had suddenly died. The house of joy instantly turned into a house of mourning. The Rabbi and the students stayed throughout the night and comforted the mourners.

In the morning, the group began their trip back to town but as soon as they were seated in the wagon, the students interrogated their Rabbi. They demanded an explanation to this bizarre series of events. How did the Rabbi know where to go and why would such an incredible occasion turn into such a great calamity? The Rabbi asked if anyone noticed what the child was named. They responded, "Yosef." The Rabbi then asked if anyone knew what was significant about yesterday's date but here the students were stumped. The Rabbi explained to them that yesterday was the *yarhzeit* (anniversary of the day of death) of a tremendously righteous individual, Rabbi Yosef Caro, the author of the Code of Jewish Law.

Rabbi Yosef Caro mastered all aspects of life and perfected himself in a brilliant way. However, when he was eight days old there was a cholera epidemic and he could not be circumcised at the ideal time, the eighth day. In his lifetime Rabbi Caro had fulfilled all the other *mitzvot* and perfected himself. "The soul of the infant that was circumcised yesterday was the soul of Rabbi Yosef Caro coming back to this world to be circumcised on the eighth day and finish his mission. After he had completed that last commandment there was nothing left for him to accomplish in this world and so his soul went back to his Maker," the Rabbi explained.

Here is a case where the person didn't do anything wrong and yet the soul had to return to the world to complete something that was lacking. Certainly if someone acted negatively in a prior lifetime that could impact their situation negatively in a next *gilgul*, but even if a person's actions in a previous life weren't necessarily negative they have an impact on the next *gilgul*. Everyone needs to come to completion, and based on their previous life, a person may need a specific challenge to help them fulfill their destiny.

Put all these possibilities together and we have some slight inkling into how the Omnipotent One directs the world to get us where we have to go. Every experience and every direction in this world is a complex tapestry leading to perfection, with trials and tribulations that often seem contrary to the good that underlies the system. When we see something bad happen, we can ask is it possible that the incident is not actually "bad"? Maybe this will save our life? Maybe this will be our next step of growth, or maybe it will allow us to earn our unique expression?

Now we understand that there are so many possibilities of the grander scheme, which includes even our actions in a previous life. Whatever the specific reason or combination thereof, remember that the Omnipotent One uses all these ways to bring us all home and bring the world to its ultimate perfection.

Application One:

Think of a difficult issue you are dealing with now or from your past. Do not choose the hardest or most trying situation. As you enter into the recollection of this challenge ask yourself one of the following questions, or something similar, that resonates with you:

1. What lesson can I learn from this difficulty to improve myself?

2. Do I have any counterproductive behaviors that may somehow be connected to this trouble?

3. What is the ideal way I want to act that would resolve my conflict?

Remind yourself of the principle that everything from Above is for the good. Recall that sometimes the challenges are in response to our negative actions or an impetus to change.

Let your mind wonder about your difficulty and keep repeating the above questions to yourself. Notice the behavior that comes into your head. If no behavior pops into your mind, just picture a way of acting that you would like to take on. Envision yourself behaving this way and see how this improved behavior can be a very positive thing for you. Contemplate the importance of the improvement and realize that if you grow from this challenge it will transform the entire experience. See yourself acting the way that you want. Feel yourself stepping into that picture of you.

Repeat this process.

Again, envision yourself acting in the ideal way you want to be and enter into that image in your mind until you are completely comfortable with the change. Resolve that you will make this change happen.

Now let yourself think about the difficulty in a new light based on the positive change that it can bring about in your life.

Endnotes

(1*) The Talmud calls this bitul Torah (the wasting of Torah study time). Rav Tzadok Hacohen says this refers to all inability to positively develop as a person should.

(2*) Most of the classical commentaries explain the system of Miracle and Nature as separate constructs and thereby related to different Divine Names of God. Our explanation in the text is based on Rabbi Eliyahu Eliezer Dessler, the author of Michtav MeEliyahu, who shows that on one level the two systems are really one. Consistent with this approach, I have explained everything under one Divine Name though technically it is only in this limited sense.

(3*) To reach the tally of 600,000 letters in the Torah we need to know how to count an individual letter since letters are often written as a combination of two letters, i.e., a Lamed is formed by combining a Kaf and a Vav. Consequently, what appears to be one letter is really two letters.

CHAPTER SEVEN

BODY AND SOUL

....

Who are we? That may sound like a crazy question but it isn't. For although every person clearly experiences their own identity, very few really recognize what is the essence of the human being.

To answer this, we need to analyze the Hebrew word for human being and understand the power of names.

The first naming in history goes back to the beginning of creation. There is a mystical teaching that there were spiritual forces (angels) who opposed the creation of mankind, protesting about human foibles. The Creator proceeded to demonstrate to these angels that mankind's wisdom is even greater than theirs. He brought the animals before the angels and asked the angels to name all the various forms of life. The angels were stumped and could not do this. Then the Creator brought the animals before Adam and asked Adam to name them. Adam demonstrated his ability and successfully named each animal. The angels were amazed and conceded to man's greatness.

This is an extremely bizarre story. Millions of people have pets and have named them without too much difficulty. It's not rocket science to name animals, so what did Adam do that was so impressive? Couldn't the angels have just randomly named the animals; call this one a moo and that one a poo and that would have taken care of it?

Actually, calling a spotted dog "Spot" or a furry creature "Fluffy" wouldn't have cut it. Names in Hebrew are not simple, randomly chosen words; rather they touch the essence of the entity. This concept is borne out in the Hebrew word for soul, *neshemah*, נשמה, which is the core of our existence. The middle two letters of that word *neshemah* spell the word *shem*, which means *name*. The name we are given represents the inner core of our being. Similarly, when Adam named the animals he wasn't scanning their random attributes but was surveying their spiritual root and their primary feature.

He called the dog *Ca'lev*, which is a conjugation of two words *Cal* and *Lev*. *Cal* means *all* and *Lev* means *heart* because the dog is *all heart*. The dog has a tremendous sense of loyalty and this characteristic is part of its unique nature. Adam named the donkey *Chamor* which is the same root as the word *Chomer* which means physical substance. This beast of burden represents the most physical, stubborn and deliberate animal. The donkey is always cold. Even in the summer it enjoys wearing a saddlebag on it for warmth. The spiritual reason for this is that blood flow represents movement, growth and connection to a higher level life Source. The donkey is the epitome of the physical, cold and static dimension. Adam called the cat *Chatul*. *Chatul* means "to cover up and to conceal" and the cat teaches us modesty in the way it covers up its excrement. The cat has pride and so it maintains a level of discretion and reservation in concealing its waste. In Modern Hebrew the word *chitul* means diaper.

And so Adam named all the creatures accordingly and the angels were dumbfounded by his tremendous wisdom.

God then asked Man to name himself. Man called himself Adam because he was formed from the *Adamah*, the earth. This is very strange reasoning. When Adam names the little doggy he scrutinizes the dog's spiritual essence to find its uniqueness and yet when naming himself, all he can focus on is that he comes from the earth? What about the fact that man has a soul which seemingly is greater than the body? If anything he should have named himself "Soul Man" a la Blues Brothers.

One reason why Adam named himself after his aspect of earthiness was to emphasize that it is impossible for a person to stand still in life. As human beings we are either going up or down. We have the capability to soar to heights but if we do not constantly climb to new levels, the earth aspect of man pulls us down.

Let's further analyze man's quality of growth as opposed to the nature of animals. The word for animal is *behaimah* (בהמה) which is a conjugation of two words, *bah* (בה) and mah (מה). *Bah* means "in it" and *mah* means "what it is." The meaning of the word *behaimah* is therefore "what it is" is already "in it." The animal is preprogrammed with its instincts and cannot do anything beyond that. Human beings, on the other hand, are all about their free-will to actualize. They are potentiality and can make themselves great or terrible. The epitome of potentiality is the earth which has the potential to produce delicious fruits or to breed weeds, and it lies barren until it is tilled and nurtured. That is the uniqueness of mankind, the only creature that has the power to actualize potential. Our spiritual greatness is that **we must make ourselves.**

Elevating the Entire Creation

To understand the importance of this ability on a deeper level we must analyze man's relationship to the rest of creation. In terms of chronology, human beings were the last created entity. Why did the Creator choose to create humans last? The answer is that humanity was designed to be the pinnacle of creation. Everything that precedes us has a specific individual aspect while we encompass and bring everything together. A bull has horns to attack and a turtle has a shell to protect him; humans are the only creatures that can make a sword and shield. On a psychological level this means that humans can emulate the characteristics of every part of creation. We can act with strength and valor like a lion, we can be swift like a deer to achieve greatness and we can be brazen like the leopard to stand up against those that would intimidate us. The Talmud says that if the Torah had not been given, we would have still learned a plethora of ethical qualities and lessons by observing the creations that preceded us. We can learn not to steal from the ant who works in a communal way with its colony. We can learn discretion from the cat who knows to conceal what should be hidden. We can learn to soothe our partner after intimacy with kind words from the way the rooster interacts with his mate after relations.

Our chronological order in the creation not only allows us to incorporate everything that came before us but it obligates us to unite everything and guide it to its ultimate goal. This was the song of the first man, Adam, when he proclaimed to all the creations, "Come let us sing praise to the Creator." We human beings have the ability and the responsibility to elevate the entire universe.

As the pinnacle of creation, humans are supposed to use everything in the world for a higher purpose. Thus our motto is: *we can use it but have no right to abuse it.* This is what the Sages mean when they say, "if a man acts properly he is called the zenith of creation, yet if he does not act meritoriously we tell him the gnat was created before him."

If a man chops down a tree to make paper on which he writes beautiful words of wisdom, he has raised the tree and helped to bring it to its higher purpose. If he writes words of hatred and antagonism on the paper, he is considered to be a tree killer. He has not used the tree to better the world in the way which he alone can do; **hence he has no right to chop it down.**

This is the idea of Jewish ecology. People don't realize the Jewish emphasis on the concept of ecology. They think Jewish ecology is recycling various food items and making *cholent,* a traditional Jewish type of stew eaten on Shabbos. Jewish ecology is actually a very real and deep concept. Certainly it manifests in requirements to keep the physical world in balance, including commandments not to chop down a fruit bearing tree, or the prohibition against wasting or destroying anything in the world. The concept of Jewish ecology in all its profundity is an all-inclusive grand plan. It is rooted in the idea that everything in the world is interconnected and man can bring all things to their purpose by using them for a higher goal to connect to and serve the Creator. And in this way make the world a better place.

Originally, Adam and Eve were commanded to be vegetarians. At the beginning of time it was not possible to use animals positively by consuming them. However, there was a change during Noah's time. The entire world then fell to a lower spiritual level and the creation was saved just because of Noah's righteousness. Noah was then given permission to eat animals. Yet there is a little known limitation here. The Talmud says that if one is not a spiritually elevated scholar he shouldn't eat meat at all!

What does meat eating have to do with spiritual prowess?

We have all heard the adage, *you are what you eat* and we have all experienced the accuracy of this statement at some time or another. We know how we feel after eating certain foods and the effect it has on us. I remember when I was living in Manhattan there were two restaurants facing each other on the same street. One was McSorley's Bar and Grill and the other was Eden's Health Food restaurant. I recall walking down the street and being struck by the different energies of the patrons of each place. The customers of the Bar and Grill were agitated and bounced around as if they were looking for a brawl while the Health food patrons were calm, meditating on alfalfa sprouts and apparently "becoming one with the world." The energy of meat is derived from the essence of the animal with all its animalistic urges. When you ingest an animal it affects you accordingly. A spiritual person will know how to take that powerful energy and direct it appropriately. However, if you don't channel that power it can actually make you more animalistic!

Additionally, since the animal is a higher-level being than mineral or plant life you need a special dispensation to use it. If you are going to use the energy of an animal for a higher purpose than the animal can achieve on its own, you have the right to kill the animal and consume it. But if you are going to eat an animal just to act like one, who says you have the right to kill it?

Man has the ability to take everything in this world and bring it to its completion by using it to perfect the world. It's not our right but rather our responsibility. Humans were created last because we include all that preceded us and we must raise the entire creation with us.

First and Last, Human Greatness Achieved in the Struggle

But this is only half the story. It's true that humans were the last entity created but they were also the first! How is that possible? The physical human body was created last but the human soul preceded all other creations. The human being contains both body and the soul. The body comes from the earthy element, *Adamah*, and so man called himself Adam. However, humans have a holy soul that is referred to as a Divine spark. The soul propels us to act righteously and strives to emulate the Omnipotent Source. And so the name Adam has another connotation. *Edmah* means, "I will emulate" as the verse in the Torah says, "*Edmah LeElyon* - I will make myself similar to the Divine." Man called himself Adam for his earth component *Adamah* and *also for his Divine spark*, his soul *Edmah LeElyon*.

Our uniqueness is precisely because of our dual nature. We are the only creations that have a Godly soul combined with a corporeal body. In this way humankind really spans and incorporates all creation. We are the first and last thing to be created and as the only entity that combines these two very different aspects we can truly transform all of reality. This is the deeper meaning of Adam's name. Our greatness is specifically because we are comprised of two opposing dimensions and we choose our way. On the one hand the earth aspect, *Adamah*, pulls us downward and on the other hand the heavenly aspect, *Edmah LeElyon*, pulls us upward. Yet **it is we that choose our path.**

We see this idea in the letters of the name Adam, אדם, which is a conjunction of two terms; the Hebrew Letter *Aleph*, א, along with the word דם, *dam*, which means blood. The letter א *Aleph* in Hebrew always signifies the spiritual, Godly component. The *Aleph* is the first letter in the Hebrew alphabet and thereby has the numerical value of one, which represents the One and Only Supreme Being. The word *Aleph* itself means the great one as in the phrase *Alupho shel Olam*, the great Master of the world. *Aleph* also means to learn, as in the Hebrew word *ulpan*, a place where you study. This refers to the highest way that we experience Divinity in this world, through learning and experiencing Torah. Still one should not mistakenly believe that the learning process is simply a matter of intellectual aptitude. The ability to connect to the Infinite is predicated on understanding that it is unfathomable. So when the letter *Aleph* is spelled backwards it forms the word *Pelah* פלא = פ-ל-א which means something astonishing and beyond imaginable. Finally, all Hebrew letters have different sounds that are enunciated with the different vowels beneath the letters. There is only one Hebrew letter that has no sound; the ineffable *Aleph*. The Divine-like aspect of man, א, *Aleph*, combines with the corporal aspect of man represented by the blood, דם, *dam*, giving us the unique creation of A-DAM, אדם; humanity.

Now since man is the only being that combines body and soul, we need to understand what is the relationship between body and soul? Why do we have both and what are we in essence?

Essentially Body or Soul?

If you were in the desert for three days without food or water and I asked you, "Are you thirsty?" What would you say? "Yes, of course I am. I am dying of thirst!" Yet that statement would not be correct. Sure your body is thirsty but your soul isn't. Let's take another example. Imagine you're busy with work or pleasure for three days straight and haven't had a chance to do even one spiritual act. Then I asked you, "Are you starving? Do you feel like you're dying?" You would look at me as if I lost my mind.

When we don't feed our bodies for even a short period of time we are devastated, yet some people go through eighty years of life without feeding their souls and don't notice a thing. If we are a combination of body and soul, how is that possible? Moreover, since a soul is a spiritual entity and greater than the physical body, we should sense the soul much more than the body, and yet the opposite is true.

We will begin to unravel the secrets of the relationship of body and soul with a mystical Talmudic teaching. The Talmud states:

"The fetus in the mother's womb has a lamp lit above its head with which it sees from one end of the earth to the other... And don't be bewildered by this, for a man may sleep in Babylon and see what is happening in Spain... and they teach the unborn child the entire Torah... but as soon as the child emerges into the air of the world an angel strikes him on his mouth causing him to forget it all."

How could an embryo learn the whole Torah and see from one end of the earth to the other? And if he is taught everything, why is he made to forget it? And finally, how does a strike on the mouth make him forget?

Let's try to unravel this mystery. The soul is the highest spiritual entity created. In its highest aspect it is called a spark of Divinity. If the soul would combine with the body in all its brilliance, it would immediately transform the body. The body would be enlightened and completely subservient to the soul. That sounds great, the only problem is that it would also mean the end of free-will and thereby reality as we know it. Since, as we have discussed, our mission in life is to choose good over evil in order to perfect ourselves, a completely enlightened body would be counterproductive at this time. Therefore, the Infinite Source lessened the power of the soul, so to speak, when connecting it to the body, to the point where the soul feels like a stranger to us. We are much more connected with our body's needs than the yearnings of our soul. That's why if I ask you after three days of not eating how you are doing, you say awful because the experience of your body in this reality is more obvious. The infinitely times more powerful voice of the soul is often not heard because God has lessened its brilliance in the present combination of body and soul. In actuality your soul has not been changed but rather you are only aware of its lower aspects. These are the aspects that are said to be contained in the body.

So now when I say that "I" see you, what exactly do I mean? Who is the "I" in the sentence? Well, I'm seeing you with my physical "I" (the eye) but it's the greater "I" that is actually seeing you. This is what we call the soul. Of course, if I don't have a physical eye, the soul (the real "I") can't see you in the same way; on the other hand, if I only have a physical eye, without the cognition of self (the soul), I could not see you at all. The body and soul are unified in a binding marriage and everything that the soul does in this reality is through the body; while without the soul, the body would be a lifeless collection of atoms.

The Soul Detached from the Limitations of the Body

However, imagine if the soul were not trapped in the body. If so, it would also not be bound by the physical laws of time and space. This may be why you often hear people who had near death experiences describe their soul leaving their body and being able to observe events that happen in different times or places. The soul is no longer limited in the physical dimension. So too when the child is in the mother's womb, the soul is not yet fully connected to the body. Consequently, it can see and understand things beyond the physical, i.e., a lamp illuminates the fetus and it knows the whole Torah. The fetus can see from one end of the world to the other as a person in a dream state, specifically because the soul is detached from the physical. When a person sleeps, certain aspects of the soul separate from the body (that is why sleep is called 1/60th of death, death being the practical complete separation of body and soul). During sleep, the lower aspects of the soul that are associated with imagination remain connected to the person's consciousness, while the higher aspects associated with cognitive thought are detached. One level of dreaming is when the thoughts and sensory impressions of the waking state are reshuffled and rearranged by the now unbridled power of the imagination left with the sleeping person. This type of dream is often analyzed from a psychological perspective because it can reveal a person's deeper thoughts and desires even on a subconscious level. However, there is a totally different level of dreams which are premonitions of future events or realities. These occur because the higher levels of the soul, which are detached from the body in the sleep state, can connect with forces in the spiritual realm. The soul may then gain awareness of some event or issue and transmit that information to the consciousness through the unrestrained power of imagination of the sleep state. These types of dreams are called 1/60th of prophecy; i.e., the slightest hint of the prophetic level. So too the fetus in the mother's womb can know spiritual knowledge and see from one end of the world to the other like a dreamer because it's soul is still unfettered by the limitations of the body.

However, when the fetus is ready to be born, the body and soul must fully unite. And so the child assumes the body/soul relationship of the present day reality where the soul is connected and married to the body, enlivening the body but becoming like a stranger in its midst. The child then automatically forgets all the Torah and spiritual insight it knew in the womb.

So if the child is going to forget it anyway, why teach the fetus everything in the first place? The answer is that since we have learned it once, in our core it remains part of us. When we go through life we are relearning what we already know. We have an affinity to truth and wisdom because it is inside us. When we hear words of truth they often ring true to us because deep down within, we have already known it. **The search for truth is not a search for something outside but rather a return to our essence.**

There is one piece still missing; why does the angel need to hit us in the mouth for us to forget everything? This angel is not a mobster working us over so we'll stay in line. Notice that the text said he strikes us specifically on the mouth. Why is that? What is the deeper meaning of hitting us on the mouth?

The mouth's unique quality is its ability to communicate and so the angel hitting us on the mouth represents **giving us the power of speech.** Human beings can think, speak and act. The thinking process represents the spiritual dimension of our soul. The action process represents the physical world where we operate. Speech combines and bridges the two. When I do an action it is obvious to the physical world. However, my thoughts are hidden and you can't experience what is happening in my internal world. The power of speech allows me to take my hidden spiritual dimension and convey it in the physical world. That's why the Hebrew word for an object is *devar*, רבד, and the Hebrew word for speech is also *devar*, רבד. Just as an object is a corporeal "thing" in the physical world, so too saying something has brought the mental concept into the physical world and made it real. And so the Sages teach us that life and death is in the power of the tongue. The words we speak become reality and so we must be extremely careful how we use this powerful gift.

At the moment of birth, the soul is merged with the body and consequently we are given the power of speech which is the channel between the two dimensions. Our soul is now trapped in our body and no longer has free access to the pure spiritual realm, we therefore forget the Torah we knew. (1*)

But who said that the body/soul relationship will always be the same as it is now? As human beings we become habituated to situations and can't imagine that they can be any different. Yet the reality is that the body/soul relationship will dramatically change in the future. In fact, **it needs to change** for us to experience higher dimensions. But to understand this deep concept we have to briefly deal with a related issue of immense proportion: what happens to us after we die?

Why the Torah Does Not Elaborate on the Details of the After-life

Interestingly, the Torah itself only briefly mentions the after-life and often only in passing. It does not explain the World to Come in great detail which has led some to mistakenly believe that there is no after-life. Though nothing could be further from the truth, we do need to understand why this crucial topic isn't discussed at greater lengths in the Torah. There are numerous reasons for this and each one reveals a different depth.

One reason is that lengthy, extravagant descriptions of reward in the after-life could encourage people **to act righteously for the wrong reasons.** It promotes a mind-set that is motivated by reward and not for the higher more selfless reasons that we should strive for.

Another approach is that the Torah details the positive responses we will experience in this life and not the next because it's easy for a religion to promise things that can't be verified. If I tell you to do something and that you will receive tremendous reward in a world you can't see, I have proven nothing. The greater authentication is to promise recompense for your actions in this world where you can test the veracity of the claim. And so the Torah has predicted in great detail the unfolding of Jewish history.

Furthermore, the idea of an after-life is actually self-evident and needs little explanation. We know all things return to their source and we understand from the law of conservation of energy that nothing is lost in the universe and so it follows that the soul must return to its eternal Source. Reward in *this world* needs discussion; the soul returning to God doesn't need much dialogue.

Although these are important reasons, there is still another rationale that we must understand to fully appreciate this issue.

When any religion or system tries to describe the pleasures of an after-life there is a serious flaw by definition. "Imagine how great heaven is" they say. "It is more delicious than all the ice cream in the world, it is more desirous that the most sensual experience." What this does in essence is to make the after-life a **revved up version of this physical reality.** Since the soul and body are united in this reality and we must think through our brain, there is no way to divest our thoughts from a physical world. We are not capable of thinking in wholly spiritual terms because we exist in a physical world! **The more I try to describe the World to Come, the more you will misconstrue it as physical.** Therefore, the less said the better. The pleasure of the World to Come is a spiritual pleasure and is much greater qualitatively than any pleasure in this physical dimension. To try to describe it in physical words will only lessen its worth in our eyes.

That being said, we will relate a bit of the sequence of the after-life and hopefully be able to glean a better understanding of this topic and how it relates to understanding the body/soul relationship.

Separation and Reunion of Body and Soul

As we have discussed, when the soul is combined with the body in this reality, its brilliance must be diminished or it will immediately transform the body and obviate any free-will and thereby the purpose of creation. However, when a person dies and the body and soul separate, the soul is given back all its original brilliance **plus the excellence it added** through the righteous acts the person did while alive.

The soul enters a state called the Soul World (*Olam Haneshamot*), also known as *Gan Eden*, the Garden of Eden. This Garden of Eden should not be confused with the physical Garden of Eden where Adam and Eve first dwelt, though the two dimensions do parallel one another. In the Soul World the soul experiences the utmost possible pleasure, greater than all the pleasures in this physical dimension combined. It is the pleasure of being able to experience the Infinite, the Divine, and the Source of all that is good, what we call God.

Now if the soul has not lived a righteous life and has become tainted, there are many possible ways to bring about the actualization of the soul. These processes include returning to this world (*gilgulim*) to remedy what was not accomplished previously, experiencing painful spiritual medicine that can rectify the person's shortcomings (*Gehinnom*), as well as numerous other spiritual consequences that may be allotted to the soul in order to realign it so that it can enter into the state of *Gan Eden*. Only the thoroughly evil will not be refined through these processes. Others will receive these spiritual remedies to allow them to participate in the Soul World. However, don't think that it pays not to be "so good" now and just get "fixed up" later; that is a grave mistake. Firstly, the response required to "fix things up" is much worse than getting it right the first time. And secondly, a person who is "fixed up" by the medicine he or she receives will not be on the same level as one who does it on their own. So although people on different levels get into *Gan Eden*, their experiences are not at all identical. It is comparable to going to the theatre where one person sits front row center while another is in the back row sitting behind a pole; both are there but their experience is very different. The Benevolent One has many ways to get us there but it is still better to do it ourselves.

Now we have discussed how the soul is refined in order to receive incredible pleasure connecting to the Infinite One. The only problem is what about the body? The body and soul worked together in this world, it is therefore impossible that the soul should experience eternal bliss while the body just rots in the grave. The body must also receive its appropriate recompense. This brings us to the extremely difficult to fathom concept of *Techiyat Hamatim*, resurrection of the dead. It's not that the concept is hard to understand, it's just that as human beings we naturally scoff at anything we don't experience in our reality. We have never seen the dead come back to life and therefore it seems bizarre.

So please allow me to make this concept a bit more digestible for you before I describe what actually happens. To get past our prejudice on this topic we must realize that we actually experience things similar to the resurrection every day but because they are common place we don't even notice. When you put a seed in the ground, it begins a type of decomposing process in the earth after which it sprouts out to create life. (2*) Why should a decomposing seed come back to life? And why doesn't that boggle your mind?

The answer is that anything we observe on a regular basis is attributed to the realm of nature. If dead people were buried, decomposed, and then "sprouted" up again and seeds didn't, you would consider that natural! Science would then come to explain how the dead come back to life. Science deals with the universe **after it is formed** and tries to understand how it functions. However, as we have discussed, the deeper reason *why* things are a certain way depends solely on the Omnipotent One's will.

In fact, it is actually more *logical* to imagine that a *once living person* buried in the earth can be reformed than it is to imagine that a *person that never existed* could be created through a sperm and egg. This though, is not the world we live in. Every day we observe people being born from the womb and vegetation springing from the earth. Consequently, these things are within our realm. The reuniting of body and soul is outside our experience and so it is hard to accept. Still we must realize that it isn't any harder for the Omnipotent One to make reality function this way or that way.

So here are the steps again:

1. The body and soul are united to function together in this reality.

2. The power of the soul is limited to provide a free-will setting.

3. When a person dies, the soul goes to the soul world, regaining all its brilliance plus what it accomplished in this reality.

4. The body returns to its components, the earth.

Here is the new part. At the end of history as we know it, the body will be reformed at a more elevated state, similar to the physical dimension the *Kabbalists* attribute to the original creation of Adam and Eve. Then the soul **in all its brilliance**, with the illumination it receives in the soul world, will be reunited with this body, transforming it immediately. The person will be at a much loftier station than ever before. Instead of the soul being a stranger in the body, the soul will begin the process of attaining dominion over the body. This type of body/soul relationship is, generally speaking, not attainable in this world. The most notable exception was Moshe. Moshe changed his body/soul relationship to the point that he did not eat or drink for forty days when he received the Torah at Mount Sinai. How could such a thing be possible? According to what we've said it should now be obvious: if the power of the soul permeates the body, it would certainly completely transform the physical. Moshe's body had become elevated to a more soul like state and although he had the ability to eat, he could also function on soul power and not eat at all (3*)!

His soul power was so apparent that the Torah tells us beams of light were exuding from his face, transforming his physical dimension. (The Hebrew words, *keren ohr* - beams of light - were mistranslated as horns which led to Michelangelo's depiction of Moshe with horns and the canard that Jews have horns).

The relationship of body and soul will go through a few more stages until finally the body will be totally subservient to the soul. The body will become almost completely soul-like and exist as an appendage to the soul (4*). In this way the body will also receive its due reward but the reward will not be limited to a mere physical payment; rather it will be the sublime connection to the Infinite by both body and soul.

The Body/Soul Relationship Changes in This Lifetime Too, Based on Your Deeds

"Alright," you say, "this is all nice for the after-life and another reality but what does this have to do with me now?" In truth, it has everything to do with you now. Since the function of the soul is to elevate the body until it is soul-like (and similarly to elevate the entire physical dimension), that task needs to be done in the present. It is only in this reality where the spiritual pulls us one way and the physical tugs us in the opposite direction that we can choose and elevate ourselves. The work must be done now, in this world, so that it can be appreciated in the future. Moreover, even though the physical will not be totally transformed until the afterlife, there is no question that there is some change now too. One who is directed by the body diminishes the power of the soul; while one that is directed by the soul empowers the soul and **even elevates the body now**. It may not be obvious immediately and it may not be obvious to all, but the spiritual person develops even a physical refinement in this life (albeit to a much lesser degree than in the future). One way that this transformation can be noticed is when morally deleterious acts give you a negative *visceral reaction* and positive spiritual acts give you a *corporeal high*. That is a sign you are transforming your body to be soul-like.

On one level the body and soul are antagonists. The pleasures of the body are meaningless to the soul and vice versa. In this reality, where there is much negativity and illusion, a person must be careful not to follow the purely physical desires of the body. And that is truly a difficult battle, for when one rises, the other falls. However, on a deeper level, the mystics reveal that the body and soul are united in their root; the soul originating from the Refined Light and the body originating from the Coarse Light. In that sense they are not antagonists at all. The body is made to be transformed by the soul like a horse is meant to be led by its rider. You are essentially a soul; but now we understand that your body too can be a reflection and extension of your soul. We just need to use the connector between the physical and spiritual dimension to elicit this transformation.

As we discussed in Chapter One, *mitzvot* literally mean connectors and they function as conduits between the physical and spiritual dimensions. The more *mitzvot* we do, the more we strengthen our soul and transform our body, now and in the future. This process also reveals the spiritual dimension of everything in the world and elevates the physical back to its holy roots.

This is our grand mission and with it we are able to enjoy the goodness that we ourselves create.

Application One:

Recognize and appreciate that you are empowered to elevate every aspect of the world. Tell yourself that you contain all elements of creation within yourself. Imagine the world stands in the balance and your positive actions can now tilt the scales. Choose an action that uses a physical item in the world. You can choose eating kosher food, preferably meat or fish for this exercise, and best on the Sabbath.

Before you eat the food, tell yourself that this fish or animal was once living in the world and you are going to use the energy from this entity to do positive things. Imagine the fish or animal's level being raised through you when you eat it. If it is the Sabbath, revel in the pleasure of the taste and think that the Omnipotent One wants you to get pleasure now. Know that this act is fulfilling a *mitzvah,* commandment.

Recognize that your pleasure is not just an individual matter but it is part of the cosmic plan. It is a positive thing for the world and in line with God's will.

After you finish your food, do a positive act (a *mitzvah*): help someone, smile and greet someone, give charity, make a blessing or say a prayer, etc., while thinking that you are **using the energy of the food to do this good act.** Realize that you have now raised the physical. Think of your physical body and recognize how it is being used for higher spiritual purposes. Meditate on this process and tell yourself repeatedly, "We can raise the physical world."

Every day look for some small positive thing that you do and return to the state that you were in during this exercise by saying, "We can elevate the physical." Think that this act is accomplishing that goal. For example, if you are showering or bathing, think how taking care of your body allows you to be positive. Before you go to sleep, think about how getting the sleep you need enables you to make the world a better place, etc.

Pick any action that involves a physical item that you will elevate. Just a few moments of this preparation for one act a day will help you align yourself and your world to a grander purpose.

Repeat this verse to yourself in English or in Hebrew: *Bechol derachecha daeihu*, which literally means, "Know God in all your ways."

This is what the Torah tells us: "In all your ways know God."

Endnotes

(1*) *This is actually the deeper meaning of the idea that Moshe had a speech impediment. In actuality Moshe's challenge in speech was because his soul was so elevated that it was less attached to his body. He therefore couldn't master speech which is a product of the soul being connected to the body. He was called Moshe because he was "drawn from the water"- Min Hamayim **Meshisuhu**. In Chassidic thought water represents physicality because it is a substance that always adapts to the form of the vessel that contains it. Moshe is drawn and separated from the physical. His soul is not sufficiently limited in the physical; he therefore can't speak properly. The Midrash says that later in his life, the words of Torah heal Moshe and he is able to speak perfectly. However, this is not because his soul became more restricted by his physical body; rather it's because his body became transformed to be more soul like. Hence Moshe existed with a different body/soul relationship than the normal person in our reality.*

(2*) *This can be seen when seeds with hard coats must be partially broken down to allow gas and water exchange, so that dormancy can be broken and germination can occur; this is called scarification. Alternatively, seeds that are planted while still in their fruits have outer husks that rot away in the ground, and the seed inside germinates the following spring.*

(3*) *Moshe's change in body/soul relationship is metaphorically represented by the idea of his removing his shoes at the burning bush and not at Mount Sinai. The soul is to be understood more like a continuum than a static entity. When the soul enters the body only the lower aspects of the* soul combine with the body; this is similar to the way a person steps into his shoes. Consequently, the body is often referred to as a "shoe." When Moshe is first at the burning bush he must remove his "shoes," i.e., he must detach from his physicality in order to experience the Divine. Later in his career, when he is more spiritually elevated, he is not ordered to remove his shoes before experiencing the Divine. Since he has transformed his physical into spiritual, the physical no longer interferes with the Divine communication; the "shoe" does not need to be removed.

(4*) We can now understand that the opinions of Maimonides and Nachmonides regarding the nature of the World to Come, which seemed to be in conflict, are not really so far apart. Nachmonides and the Kabbalists explain that the World to Come is after the resurrection and consequently would have some physical component while Maimonides speaks about the World to Come in strictly spiritual terms. However, once we understand that the body is transformed to be soul–like, it is not considered physical at all. It can be what the Sages call the Levush or the Chaluk DeRabbanin, the outer aspect of the soul itself which exists, according to all, on the spiritual level. Therefore, according to everyone, in the final analysis, the World to Come is completely spiritual.

BIO BLURB

Rabbi Ingber lived in Israel for twenty years, where he studied with leading scholars and taught in many *yeshivot* and seminaries, including Aish Hatorah, Bircas Hatorah, Shearim Women's College, Hebrew University Beis Midrash program and the Jerusalem Kollel, to name a few. He also founded an outreach training organization for Rabbis called Talmidei Aharon (later known as Ner LeElef) where he trained over 300 people who now serve in Jewish communities throughout the world.

Rabbi Ingber attended NYU and has a master degree from Newport University in Counseling Psychology. He served as a staff member at the Shotz Family Counseling Center in Israel and combines his knowledge of psychology, Neuro-Linguistic programming, hypnotherapy and other counseling systems with his deep understanding of Torah and spirituality to translate wisdom into personal growth.

An accomplished musician, he was a member of the Diaspora Yeshiva Band and formed his own band with Lynyrd Skynyrd drummer, Artimus Pyle, called *Remez*. He has two popular CD's, including the critically acclaimed CD *Safire Sky*.

After living in Israel, he and his family moved to Montreal where he founded the Montreal Jewish Experience to connect Jews back to their heritage with exciting classes and programs. They then relocated by "flying south" to settle in Atlanta, Georgia where he is the founding rabbi and spiritual leader of The Kehilla.

He is also the director of the young adult outreach program, *Tribe Atlanta* and the *Inner Spark*, for people of all backgrounds to learn about the universal spiritual laws.

Rabbi Ingber lives in Sandy Springs with his wife and children.

Printed in the United States
By Bookmasters